complete

italian

complete
italian

First published in Great Britain in 1997 by
Hamlyn, a division of Octopus Publishing Group Ltd
2–4 Heron Quays, London E14 4JP

Reprinted 2001

ISBN 0 600 60525 6

NOTES

Standard level spoon measurements are used in all recipes.

Eggs should be medium to large unless otherwise stated.
The USDA advises that eggs should not be consumed raw. This
book contains dishes made with raw or lightly cooked eggs. It is
advisable for more vulnerable people such as pregnant and nursing
mothers, invalids, the elderly, babies, and young children to avoid
uncooked or lightly cooked dishes made with eggs. Once
prepared, these dishes should be kept refrigerated and used
quickly.

Meat and poultry should be cooked thoroughly. To test if poultry
is cooked, pierce the flesh through the thickest part with a skewer
or fork—the juices should run clear, never pink or red. Do not re-
freeze poultry that has been frozen previously and thawed.
Do not re-freeze a cooked dish that has been frozen previously.

Milk should be whole milk unless otherwise stated.

Nut and Nut Derivatives
This book includes dishes made with nuts and nut derivatives. It
is advisable for those with known allergic reactions to nuts and
nut derivatives and those who may be potentially vulnerable to
these allergies, such as pregnant and nursing mothers, invalids,
the elderly, babies, and children to avoid dishes made with nuts
and nut oils. It is also wise to check the labels of pre-prepared
ingredients for the possible inclusion of nut derivatives.

Pepper should be freshly ground black pepper unless otherwise
stated.

Fresh herbs should be used, unless otherwise stated. If
unavailable, use dried herbs as an alternative, but halve the
quantities stated.

Ovens should be pre-heated to the specified temperature—if
using a fan-assisted oven, follow the manufacturer's instructions
for adjusting the time and the temperature.

Vegetarians should ensure that cheeses are made with vegetarian
rennet. There are vegetarian forms of Parmesan, feta, Cheddar,
Cheshire, Monterey Jack, dolcelatte, goats' cheeses, and many
others.

Contents

Introduction

It is often said that whereas we all have to eat to live, the Italians live to eat! This is an affectionate and amusing observation underlying an essential truth. It is also an indication of the sheer passion which Italian food inspires in its own land. Internationally, the cuisine is regarded as second to none – although the limited range of dishes that is familiar outside the country belies the rich variety that is available within Italy itself. Visitors to Italy have taken their enthusiasm for its food back to their home countries. That is why Italian restaurants are so enduringly popular. New ones are opening all the time, and cater to all tastes – from the smart pizzerias and bustling cafés favoured by trendy young things to classic *ristorantes* serving traditional dishes.

Cooking Italian food

You don't have to eat out in restaurants to experience the joys of Italian food. It is surprisingly easy to cook delicious dishes in your own home. This is because Italians have never lost sight of their basic principles in cooking – which means top-quality ingredients simply prepared. The food has generally been known for its rustic simplicity, with pizza and pasta leading the field in popularity. Deep Fried Artichokes, Octopus and Tomato Salad or Swordfish Palermo-style are all very easy to prepare and will make memorable meals, whether you are cooking for your family or entertaining guests. The game dishes provide authentic Italian flavors that will be appreciated by the most sophisticated of palates; and the glorious desserts, whether rich and creamy, or cool and refreshing, will provide a fitting finale to a special evening's dinner.

Eating and relaxing

Modern life is often stressful and fast-moving, so if some of the more relaxed aspects of Italian eating styles can be emulated, so much the better. Family meals in Italy have a light-hearted atmosphere. The cooking found in many households is often far superior to anything served in restaurants. The main meal of the day is an important social occasion, it is the time when all the family can get together and share the day's news and gossip while enjoying wonderful home-cooked food. A typical family meal can go on for hours and is really very flexible. It usually consists of a *minestra* (soup, pasta dish, or risotto) followed by a main course (*piatto de mezzo*). This might be meat, fish, or poultry with one or two vegetables. If the *minestra* course is not included, then an *antipasto* course is served – this could be a mixture of salamis, some stuffed vegetables, or a mixed seafood salad. Often a raw salad

vegetable is served – it is not unusual for a dish of shelled fava beans to appear. These are eaten raw, dipped in salt. The meal often ends with fresh fruit in season, sometimes cheese, and is rounded off with a small cup of good, strong espresso coffee. If the meal is quite special, there may be a more complicated dessert such as a luscious cake or pie or a cooling ice cream. The Italian cook usually shops for these family meals in colorful local food markets and specialist grocery stores. These also provide an endless source of social interest as well as fresh produce in splendid profusion.

Italian ingredients

Nowadays we are very fortunate to have well-stocked supermarkets that offer a dazzling range of Italian ingredients. These enable the average cook to achieve the true flavour of a classic recipe. You can buy many good quality Italian ingredients without going near a specialist

food store. There are wonderful Italian olive oils, fresh herbs, regional cheeses, tomato purées, shining olives, plain or stuffed, cans of tomatoes, jars of pesto, artichoke hearts, sun-dried tomatoes, capers, cans of anchovies, and all kinds of pasta, fresh and dry. Pasta can be a subject of great debate among Italian food lovers. Many are convinced that fresh pasta is far superior to dried. Fortunately, fresh pasta is easy to make at home, with or without a pasta machine. A machine is simple to use and will give you a more uniform result, but it is perfectly possible to make excellent pasta and to cut the dough by hand. Whatever method you use, it is well worth the effort. The salad and vegetable shelves of major supermarkets are excellent sources of fresh herbs (including those growing in pots), wonderful salad leaves, and Italian vegetables flown in farm-fresh. Even fashionable vegetables like cavalo nero, the deliciously flavoured Italian cabbage, are increasingly available at quite reasonable prices. If you plan to do a lot of Italian cooking, then a well-stocked pantry is invaluable. You will find it useful to refer to the special features on these and other Italian ingredients that are included throughout the book.

The flowering of Italian cuisine

Italian cooking is incredibly diverse. Technically, there is no "Italian" food as such; more accurately the cuisine is a collection of classic regional dishes. There are many proud

> *"The cuisine is a colorful patchwork of local specialities, quirky recipes, and customs that would take years to explore fully."*

names preceding Italy's great dishes — Venetian, Roman, Sicilian, Bolognese, and Neapolitan for example. These traditions of cooking have developed over many centuries and their sources are anchored in several cultures including Roman, Byzantine, and Greek. The main outpouring of creativity occurred during the Renaissance however. Every aspect of life was affected during this period — arts, music, and food alike. Traders introduced exotic ingredients from other parts of the world, and this new interest in food meant that cookery became an important skill. In Florence, Milan, and Rome, the great regional ruling families gave banquets to impress each other with the splendour of their palaces — and their cooks vied to use the new ingredients that arrived in Venice and Genoa on the spice route from the East Indies. Florence was the great center of Italian cuisine and the Medicis gave wildly extravagant feasts. Caterina de' Medici took the finest Italian chefs with her on her marriage to the French Dauphin in 1553, and she is credited with introducing the art of fine cuisine to the French nation!

Regional variations

Very few visitors to Italy ever get to know the full complexity of its regional differences. The cuisine is a colorful patchwork of local specialities, quirky recipes, and customs that would take years to explore fully. It is much easier to appreciate the scope of Italian food by comparing north and south. The north is heavily industrialized and affluent, with fertile soil and a temperate climate while the south is hot, arid, and more rural. If you wanted a really quick way of distinguishing the difference between north and south, simply check out the pasta. In the north they eat flat pasta, freshly made with eggs; in the south the tubular variety is commonly used. The northerners cook with butter while the southerners use olive oil.

In general, southern flavours are much stronger because of the use of herbs and aromatics, particularly in sauces.

Rice dishes are characteristic of northern Italian cooking — this is because the Po valley provides abundant supplies of arborio rice, which is perfect for making the region's splendid risottos. One of Lombardy's classic dishes, Risotto Milanese, is justifiably world famous. Other well-known products of the north are Parmesan cheese and prosciutto ham, both from Parma. These two are linked by their methods of production. The whey left over from making the cheese is fed to the Parma pigs. The meat from these pigs is then carefully salted and dried, creating a delicately flavoured ham.

Italy is almost completely surrounded by the sea and local fish are a dominant feature of many regional cuisines. Venice is famous for its red and grey mullet, squid, shrimp, and mussels. In the north excellent freshwater fish – especially eels – are caught in the Lombardy lakes. The southern coastline and the islands of Sardinia and Sicily are famous for their picturesque fishing villages. The boats catch tuna, sardines, swordfish, and all kinds of shellfish which are extensively used in local pasta dishes, sauces, stews, soups, and salads. Abundant supplies of tomatoes, garlic, herbs, and anchovies in the south give their dishes their typical, highly aromatic flavours. Naples is the culinary capital of the south and is believed to be the original home of both pizza and modern day ice cream. Pizzas are baked in open brick ovens and are mostly eaten as casual snacks. Mozzarella, the cheese used for pizza toppings, has been made for hundreds of years in the surrounding countryside of Campania. Its excellent melting qualities make it perfect for pizzas and many other cooked dishes.

Wine

Some years Italy is the largest wine producer in the world. With wines produced in virtually every region of the country, a huge range of Italian wines is now available for export and this is increasing all the time. Of these wines, the better quality ones are enlarging their share of the market, giving lovers of Italian wine ample choice whatever their taste and pocket.

There are various categories of classification: the DOC system rules out non-traditional grapes, and ensures the quality of the wine. DOC stands for *Denominazione di Origine Controllata*. Labels bearing the initials IGT denote *Indicazione Geografica Tipica*, which is the equivalent of *Vin de Pays* in France. However, there are very fine, and expensive, wines being produced in Italy outside the restrictions of the DOC system; the first of these were known as "Super Tuscans" but producers in other areas have followed suit. These are labelled *Vino da Tavola*, "table

wine" and they are more modern wines, of high quality.

The robust reds from Piedmont include Barola, one of Italy's greatest wines, made from the Nebbiolo grape and with a complex flavor, Barbaresco, and Gattinara. All are good with meat and game, wild mushroom risottos, and cheese. Perhaps Italy's most famous wine, Chianti Classico hails from Tuscany. Chianti is a robust red and an excellent wine to drink with roasts, grills, and game dishes.

Veneto, the region which stretches from Venice and Verona to the Alps, produces Valpolicella, a lighter red which is an ideal partner for pasta and pizza, as well as roast meats. The white Soave is from the same region, and is one of its most famous wines.

Another famous white wine, this one from the region south-east of Rome, is Frascati which is extremely popular. It is ideal for drinking with summer salads and dining al fresco. Asti, from Piedmont, is a light, sweet, sparkling wine, particularly good with rich dried-fruit desserts like plum pudding.

Fortified wines such as the well-known Marsala from Sicily can be sweet or dry. The dry version is drunk as an apéritif and the sweet as a dessert wine, and it is also used to flavor desserts such as zabaglione.

Fresh stock recipes

You will find it very useful to refer to these basic recipes as they are required for many of the recipes throughout the book. A good stock is easy, satisfying, and cheap to make, and uses only a few basic ingredients. It is a pity to resort to stock cubes when the flavour of a delicious fresh broth is far preferable. If you are making fish stock you should be able to find the bones you need at your local fish market.

Once made, the stocks can be frozen when cooled.

Freeze them in small batches in plastic containers or ice cube trays. When frozen, the cubes can be transferred to clearly labelled plastic bags for ease of storage.

Every cook should be aware that a few basic rules are necessary in the making of a good stock. If you follow them, you will find that your finished dishes will taste much better.

Stock should always be simmered extremely gently, or it will evaporate too quickly and become cloudy. Never add salt to the stock as simmering will reduce it and concentrate the flavor. This will affect the flavor of the finished dish. Any scum that rises to the surface should be removed as it appears, otherwise it will spoil the colour and flavor of the stock.

Beef stock

Place 1½ lb cubed boneless beef shank, 2 chopped onions, 2–3 chopped carrots, 2 chopped celery sticks, 1 bay leaf, 1 bouquet garni (made with 2 parsley sprigs, 2 thyme sprigs, and 1 bay leaf), and 4–6 black peppercorns in a large saucepan. Cover with 6 cups water.

Slowly bring to the boil, and immediately reduce the heat to a slow simmer. Cover with a close-fitting lid and simmer for 4 hours, removing any scum from the surface. Strain the stock through a cheesecloth-lined sieve and leave to cool before refrigerating.

Makes about 5 cups
Preparation time: 15 minutes
Cooking time: about 4½ hours

Chicken stock

Chop a cooked chicken carcass into 3 or 4 pieces and place in a large saucepan with the raw giblets and trimmings. Add 1 roughly chopped onion, 2 roughly chopped large carrots, 1 roughly chopped celery stick, 1 bay leaf, a few lightly crushed parsley stalks, and 1 thyme sprig. Cover with 6 cups cold water.

Bring to the boil, removing any scum from the surface. Lower the heat and simmer for 2–2½ hours. Strain the stock through a cheesecloth-lined sieve and leave to cool.

Bring slowly to just below boiling point. Simmer for 20 minutes, removing any scum from the surface. Strain the stock through a cheesecloth-lined sieve and leave to cool completely before refrigerating.

Makes about 6 cups
Preparation time: 10 minutes
Cooking time: 20 minutes

Vegetable stock

This recipe for vegetable stock can be varied to your own taste, and adapted according to what vegetables you have available. For example, you can try adding some bulb fennel for a mild aniseed flavor, or a sliver of orange zest for an added lift. The addition of tomatoes will give the finished stock extra richness of flavor and color. Remember to avoid using any floury root vegetables as they will cause the stock to become cloudy.

Place 1 lb chopped mixed vegetables – for example, equal quantities of carrots, leeks, celery, onion, and mushrooms – with 1 garlic clove, 6 peppercorns, and 1 bouquet garni (made with 2 parsley sprigs, 2 thyme sprigs and 1 bay leaf) in a large saucepan, and cover with 4 cups water.
  Bring to the boil and simmer gently for 30 minutes, skimming off any scum when necessary. Strain, and cool the stock completely before refrigerating.

Makes about 4 cups
Preparation time: 5–10 minutes
Cooking time: about 45 minutes

Makes about 4 cups
Preparation time: 5–10 minutes
Cooking time: about 2½ hours

Fish stock

It is important to remember that when you are purchasing the bones for this stock, you should avoid the bones of oily fish. It is also very important that the stock does not boil.

Place 3 lb fish trimmings in a large saucepan with 1 sliced onion, the white part of 1 small leek, 1 celery stick, 1 bay leaf; 6 parsley stalks; 10 whole peppercorns, and 2 cups dry white wine . Cover with 6 cups cold water.

Cook's Tools

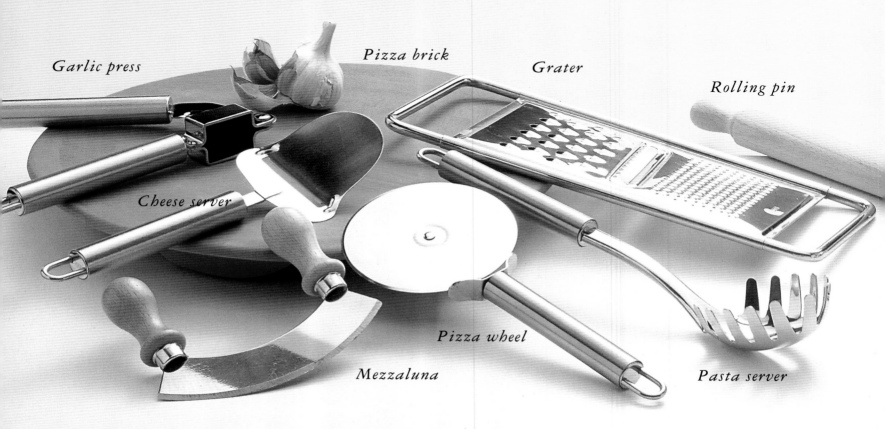

Garlic press

Pizza brick

Grater

Rolling pin

Cheese server

Pizza wheel

Mezzaluna

Pasta server

Garlic press
Used to crush garlic cloves to a fine pulp, which speeds up cooking and releases all the garlic flavor into food.

Cheese server
Generally made of stainless steel and used at the table for cutting thin slices of firm, hard cheese and transferring them to individual plates. It can also be used for slicing shavings from a block of Parmesan.

Mezzaluna
A half moon-shaped blade, with one or two handles used for chopping mushrooms, herbs, etc. using a rocking motion. Mezzalunas sometimes come with their own wooden chopping bowl.

Pizza brick
Usually made of terracotta, this is used to bake pizzas and flat breads instead of a baking sheet. It retains the heat well and crisps the bottom of the pizza during baking. Traditional pizzas are always baked on a pizza brick. The brick should have a raised foot to allow an easy grip when removing it from the oven.

Pizza wheel
A multi-purpose implement for cutting out pizzas, pastry, and pasta. When choosing a cutter, make sure that the wheel turns freely.

Pasta server
A long-handled spoon, made of stainless steel or plastic, used for transferring pasta from the saucepan to the serving dish. This useful gadget has teeth which grip long strands of pasta firmly but lightly, while the water drains away through the hole in the middle.

Grater
Available as a flat sheet or in a box shape, which is more stable when in use, graters have a selection of different-sized perforations for grating a variety of items

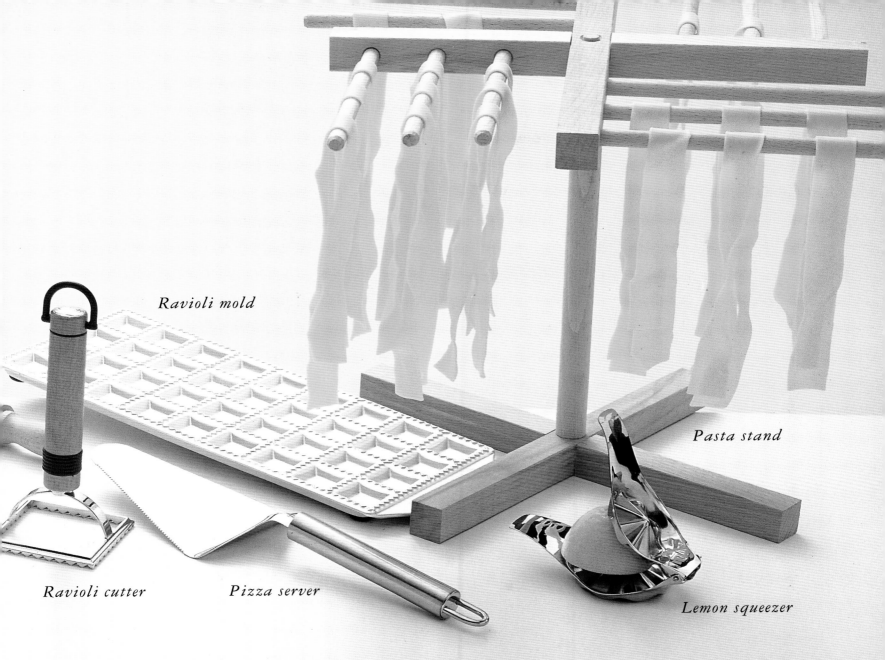

Ravioli mold

Pasta stand

Ravioli cutter

Pizza server

Lemon squeezer

from spices and citrus zest, to vegetables and cheese.

Rolling pin

Used for rolling out pasta, bread dough, and pastry, rolling pins are usually made of wood or marble. Choose a heavy rolling pin, as this makes rolling easier, and always flour the rolling pin lightly every time you use it to stop it sticking.

Always wipe a rolling pin before putting it away.

Ravioli cutter

A fluted-edged metal cutter with a wooden handle, used for stamping out individual raviolis or other flat pasta shapes. It is made in variety of shapes and sizes.

Ravioli mold

A metal tray with a series of

indentations for cutting out ravioli shapes in large numbers. A small rolling pin is sometimes provided with a ravioli mold.

Pizza server

Wide-bladed, usually made of stainless steel, and used for transferring pizzas from the serving dish to individual plates. It can also double as a pie server.

Pasta stand

This wooden stand for drying homemade pasta is a must for serious home pasta-makers and sweeps away all the awkward Heath Robinson methods of precariously drying pasta over the backs of chairs and broom handles. The stand comes apart and can be packed away in its box for ease of storage.

Lemon squeezer

These are available in a wide range of shapes and sizes. The lemon squeezer pictured above is designed for use at the table, pressing the juice from the lemon slice or half lemon between the two curved surfaces, and must be used over the food. The traditional lemon squeezer always has a saucer to catch the juice.

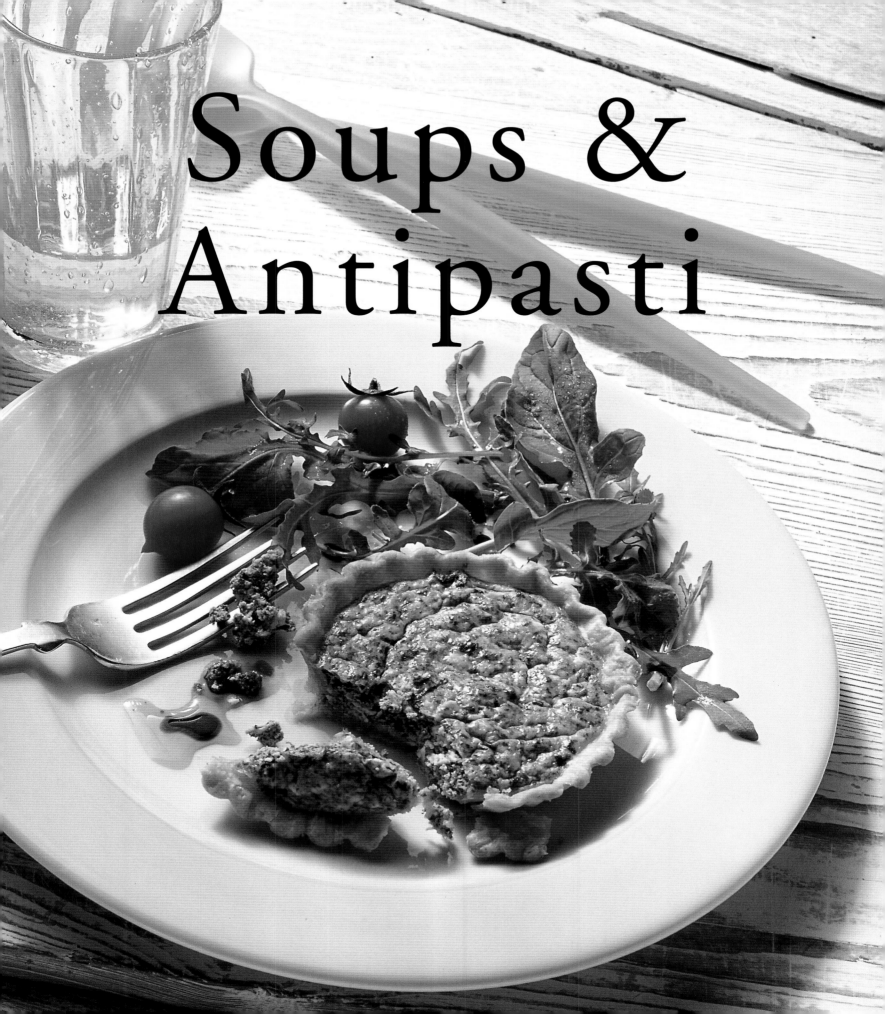

Soups & Antipasti

Minestrone Verde

with red pesto

¼ cup dry white or cannellini beans, soaked
overnight
3 tablespoons olive oil
2 garlic cloves, crushed
1 celery stick, finely chopped
2 leeks, cut into rounds
3 tomatoes, skinned and chopped
3 tablespoons chopped Italian parsley
1 tablespoon chopped basil
1 tablespoon chopped chives
½ cup green beans, cut into 1-inch pieces
4 oz asparagus, cut into 1-inch pieces
¾ cup shelled fava beans, defrosted if frozen, skinned
½ cup shelled peas, fresh or frozen
4 cups Vegetable or Chicken Stock (see pages 10
and 11) or boiling water
½ cup long-grain rice
6 oz fresh spinach
salt and pepper
¼ cup finely grated Parmesan cheese, to serve

Red pesto
2 garlic cloves, chopped
2 tablespoons basil leaves
3 tablespoons pine nuts
8 sun-dried tomatoes in oil, drained
½ cup extra virgin olive oil
2 tablespoons grated Parmesan cheese

drain and rinse the dried beans, place in a saucepan and cover with cold water. Bring to a boil, reduce the heat and simmer for 45 minutes–1 hour or until tender. Remove from the heat and set aside in their cooking liquid.

to make the pesto, place the garlic, basil, pine nuts, and sun-dried tomatoes in a food processor or blender and process until finely chopped. With the motor running, gradually add the extra virgin olive oil in a thin stream until blended. Scrape into a bowl, stir in the Parmesan, and season to taste with salt and pepper. Set aside.

heat the oil in a large saucepan, add the garlic, celery, and leeks and cook gently for 5–10 minutes until softened. Add the tomatoes with half of the herbs, season with salt and pepper, and cook for about 12–15 minutes until the tomatoes are soft.

add the green beans, asparagus, fresh fava beans, and peas, if using. Cook for 1–2 minutes, then add the stock or water. Bring to the boil and boil rapidly for 10 minutes. Add the rice, the cooked white or cannellini beans and their cooking liquid, and the spinach (and the frozen fava beans and peas, if using) and cook for 10 minutes. Adjust the seasoning to taste and stir in the remaining herbs. Serve each bowl of soup with a spoonful of pesto, and sprinkle with the Parmesan.

Serves 4–6
Preparation time: *30 minutes, plus soaking*
Cooking time: *about 2 hours*

Pumpkin Soup

The bright orange pumpkin is popular in Italian cooking and is used as both a fruit and a vegetable. Pumpkins have a delicate flavour and are low in calories.

¼ cup butter or margarine

1½ lb pumpkin, peeled, deseeded and cut into large pieces

½ cup warm water

¼ teaspoon grated nutmeg

pinch of dried thyme

5 cups milk

¼ cup long-grain rice

salt and white pepper

Croutons

3–4 slices white or brown bread, crusts removed

3–4 tablespoons olive oil

melt the butter or margarine in a large saucepan. Add the pumpkin. Stir well and cook over a low to moderate heat for 10 minutes. Add the warm water, nutmeg, and thyme, with salt and pepper to taste. Cover and cook quickly over a high heat until the pumpkin is soft.

purée the pumpkin mixture in a food processor or blender (in batches if necessary) with a little milk until smooth. Alternatively, rub through a sieve. Scrape the purée into a clean saucepan.

add the remaining milk and the rice to the pumpkin purée in the pan. Stir well and cook, covered, for 30 minutes or until the rice is tender. Stir from time to time.

make the croutons by cutting the bread slices into ½-inch cubes. Heat the oil in a frying pan, add the bread and fry, turning frequently, until golden brown. Using a slotted spoon transfer the croutons to paper towels to drain. Serve the pumpkin soup in warmed bowls garnished with the croutons.

Serves 6
Preparation time: *about 10 minutes*
Cooking time: *40–45 minutes*

La Ribollita

This is one of Tuscany's most famous soups. Its Italian name "ribollita" means reboiled, and refers to the fact that in the old days the soup was reheated and served day after day.

1 cup dried cannellini beans, soaked overnight

6 tablespoons olive oil

2 onions, roughly chopped

2 carrots, thickly sliced into rings

2 celery sticks, roughly chopped

2 potatoes, roughly chopped

4 tablespoons passata (Italian puréed tomatoes)

1 medium Savoy cabbage, finely shredded

4 cups water

pinch of dried rosemary

pinch of dried thyme

4 slices stale white bread, crusts removed

salt and pepper

drain the beans and rinse under cold running water. Place them in a large saucepan, cover with fresh cold water, and bring to a boil. Boil rapidly for 10 minutes, then lower the heat and half cover with a lid. Simmer for 1½ hours or until the beans are tender, skimming off the scum and adding water as necessary.

transfer about half of the beans and their liquid to a food processor or blender and work until smooth. Alternatively, rub through a sieve.

heat 4 tablespoons of the oil in a saucepan, add the vegetables, and cook gently, stirring frequently, for 10 minutes until softened.

add the puréed tomatoes and beans and stir well to mix, then add the cabbage, water, rosemary, thyme, and salt and pepper to taste. Bring to the boil, then cover and simmer gently for 1 hour.

tear the bread into the soup and add the whole beans and their liquid. Stir well to mix, then simmer for 10 minutes longer. Check the seasoning. Serve hot, drizzled with the remaining oil.

Serves 6
Preparation time: *20 minutes, plus soaking*
Cooking time: *2½ hours*

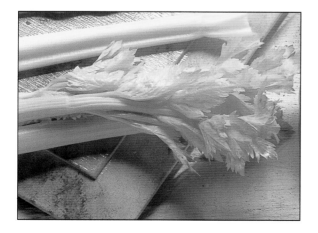

Spinach and Broccoli Soup

2 tablespoons olive oil
¼ cup butter
1 onion, diced
1 garlic clove, chopped
2 potatoes, chopped
1 small head broccoli, chopped
10 oz spinach, washed and chopped
3 cups Chicken or Vegetable Stock (see pages 10 and 11)
½ cup Gorgonzola cheese, crumbled into small pieces
juice of ½ lemon
½ teaspoon grated nutmeg
salt and pepper
½ cup toasted pine nuts, to garnish
warm crusty bread, to serve

heat the oil and butter in a saucepan, add the onion and garlic, and sauté for 3 minutes.

add the chopped potatoes, broccoli, spinach, and stock, bring to a boil and simmer for 15 minutes.

add the Gorgonzola to the soup with the lemon juice, nutmeg, and salt and pepper to taste. This soup can be liquidized or left with chunky pieces according to taste. Garnish with the toasted pine nuts and serve with warm crusty bread.

Serves 4
Preparation time: *10 minutes*
Cooking time: *20 minutes*

Tuscan Bean Soup

In the past the country people made a version of this soup by putting the beans in a large round-bottomed chianti bottle, filling it up with oil and water, garlic and herbs, and leaving it overnight in the embers of the fire.

2 tablespoons olive oil
4 shallots, chopped
2 garlic cloves, chopped
¼ lb salt pork, diced
1 carrot, diced
2 celery sticks, diced
½ red bell pepper, cored, deseeded and diced
14 oz can borlotti beans, drained and rinsed
4 cups Chicken Stock (see page 10)
1 bay leaf
1 teaspoon chopped oregano
1 teaspoon chopped marjoram
handful of Italian parsley, chopped
salt and black pepper
extra virgin olive oil, to finish

heat the oil in a saucepan, add the shallots, garlic, bacon, carrot, celery, and red pepper and cook, stirring occasionally, for 5 minutes.

add the beans, stock, bay leaf, oregano, and marjoram, bring to a boil and simmer for 15 minutes. Skim off any scum that may come from the beans.

taste and season well. Finally, just before serving, remove the bay leaf and add the chopped parsley.

ladle the soup into warmed bowls and drizzle each one with a little extra virgin olive oil.

Serves 4
Preparation time: *10 minutes*
Cooking time: *25 minutes*

Zuppa di Zucchini *al Basilico*

4 tablespoons olive oil
2 tablespoons butter, softened
1 large onion, finely chopped
1½ lb zucchini, sliced
2 potatoes, diced
5 cups Chicken Stock (see page 10)
12 basil leaves, finely chopped
1 garlic clove, finely chopped
2 eggs
4 tablespoons grated Parmesan cheese
salt and pepper

To serve
6 slices crusty bread
grated Parmesan cheese (optional)

heat the oil and half of the butter in a deep heavy saucepan and fry the onion over a low heat until soft but not colored.

add the zucchini, mix well, and fry over a low heat for about 10 minutes.

add the potatoes to the pan and stir over a moderate heat for 3–4 minutes, then add the chicken stock. Bring slowly to a boil, cover the pan, and simmer over a moderate heat for 40 minutes. Purée the soup in a food processor or blender (in batches if necessary) until smooth. Alternatively, rub the soup through a sieve.

put the basil in a large bowl with the garlic, eggs, the remaining butter, and the Parmesan, then beat with a wooden spoon or whisk. Trickle the soup into the beaten egg mixture and season with salt and pepper. Return the soup to the pan and reheat gently over a low heat.

place a slice of crusty bread at the bottom of each warmed soup bowl and pour over the hot soup. Serve immediately, sprinkled with Parmesan if liked.

Serves 6
Preparation time: *15 minutes*
Cooking time: *1 hour*

Country Bread
with olive oil and garlic

This very simple antipasto is traditionally made with sourdough bread at olive harvest time in late fall. Bruschetta is its best-known name outside Tuscany, but locally it is also called fettunta.

4 large slices country bread
2 large garlic cloves, halved
8 tablespoons extra virgin olive oil
coarse sea salt

toast the bread on both sides under a preheated broiler until light golden. While the bread is still warm, rub one side with the cut sides of the garlic.

place the bread on a plate and drizzle 2 tablespoons of the olive oil over each slice. Sprinkle with salt to taste and serve immediately.

Serves 2–4
Preparation time: *5 minutes*
Cooking time: *4 minutes*

clipboard: To match the flavor of the first pressing of Tuscan olives, use the best extra virgin olive oil you can afford; the fruity green olive oil from Lucca is one of the best.

Tuscans like to toast their bread over an open fire – the word bruschetta comes from *bruscare*, meaning "roast over coals."

You can do this too, or you could chargrill it on a cast-iron grill pan on top of the stove. Look for a close-textured bread such as *pugliese* – it is better for bruschetta than the open-textured ciabatta.

Crostini

2 red bell peppers
8 slices ciabatta bread
2 garlic cloves, peeled
small handful of Italian parsley, chopped
5 tablespoons olive oil
3 oz black olives, pitted
½ cup goat cheese, crumbled
salt and pepper

broil the red peppers on a foil-lined broiling pan under a preheated broiler for 15–20 minutes, turning frequently until charred on all sides. Transfer to a plastic bag and leave until cool enough to handle.

toast the bread on both sides under a preheated broiler until golden brown.

rub the garlic over the bread on one side; the bread acts as a grater and the garlic is evenly spread over the bread. Sprinkle with parsley and salt and drizzle with olive oil.

peel and deseed the peppers and cut the flesh into strips.

mix together the red peppers, olives, and crumbled goat cheese and season with pepper.

spread the mixture evenly over the toasted bruschetta and place under a preheated low broiler for 2 minutes until the cheese is just melted. Serve immediately.

Serves 4
Preparation time: *10 minutes*
Cooking time: *20–25 minutes*

clipboard: Sliced tomatoes, sprinkled with oregano and pepper, make another very good crostini topping.

Mixed Antipasti

16 asparagus spears, cooked and cooled

4 slices smoked salmon

7 oz can tuna, drained

8 oz can artichoke hearts, drained

4 oz can sardines

4 oz mozzarella cheese, sliced

2 hard-boiled eggs, shelled and quartered

1 cup cooked peeled shrimp

½ cup black olives

olive oil

salt and pepper

lemon wedges, to serve

wrap each slice of smoked salmon loosely around the middle of 3–4 spears of asparagus.

arrange all the other ingredients decoratively on a large platter. Season with salt and pepper and drizzle a little oil over the fish. Cover closely and refrigerate until required.

serve with lemon wedges.

Serves 4
Preparation time: *20 minutes, plus chilling*

clipboard: The original Italian name for this dish is *Antipasto Volente*. *Volente* is roughly translated as "how it comes," meaning you can use any selection of cold food that you like. Fish and shellfish, slices of cheese, Parma ham or salami, and fruits such as slices of melon and sliced fresh figs are typically Italian and combine very well.

Grilled Radicchio

with pears and Gorgonzola

This is an unusual and delicious appetizer and has a lovely combination of flavors. It is also excellent cooked over the barbecue in summer.

4 ripe pears
juice and finely grated zest of 2 oranges
4 tablespoons clear honey
4 small heads radicchio, cut into quarters
1 tablespoon walnut oil
4 oz Gorgonzola cheese, crumbled
pepper

cut each pear into quarters lengthways and remove the cores. Place the pears in a single layer on a large double-thickness sheet of aluminum foil, turning up the edges slightly. Mix the orange juice, zest, and honey in a bowl. Pour over the pears. Bring up the edges of the aluminum foil and press together to seal. Place the parcel in a heavy frying pan and cook over a moderate heat for about 15–20 minutes, or until the pears are tender.

start to cook the radicchio about 6 minutes before the pears are ready. Brush the radicchio quarters with the walnut oil and cook under a preheated broiler for 2–3 minutes on each side.

divide the pears and their cooking juices between 4 plates. Add 4 radicchio quarters to each portion, then sprinkle with the crumbled Gorgonzola and a little pepper. Serve immediately.

Serves 4
Preparation time: *5 minutes*
Cooking time: *15–20 minutes*

Deep-fried Globe Artichokes

You do not have to use baby artichokes for this dish. If you want to use larger artichokes pre-cook them before deep-frying. Baby artichokes are available from good supermarkets or specialist stores.

12 baby globe artichokes
1 lemon, halved
4 tablespoons flour
vegetable oil, for deep-frying
salt and pepper
lemon wedges, to garnish

trim the artichokes and cut each one lengthways in half or quarters depending on their size. Rub all over the cut surfaces with the halved lemon.

heat 2 inches vegetable oil in a deep frying pan until it reaches 350–375°F, or until a cube of bread browns in 30 seconds.

season the flour with salt and pepper, and use to coat the artichokes, then deep-fry them in batches for 1–2 minutes until crisp and golden. Drain on paper towels. Serve sprinkled with salt and garnished with lemon wedges.

Serves 4
Preparation time: *20 minutes*
Cooking time: *1–2 minutes each batch*

Panzanella

Traditionally panzanella was a way for frugal cooks to use up stale country bread, but now it has become quite fashionable as an antipasto or primo piatto *in its own right. It is a salad for days when tomatoes are at their sweetest.*

4 thick slices country bread
1 red onion, finely chopped
1 large garlic clove, finely chopped
½ cucumber, peeled and diced
½ cup extra virgin olive oil
2 tablespoons red wine vinegar
4 ripe plum tomatoes, roughly chopped
2 tablespoons roughly chopped Italian parsley
2 tablespoons basil leaves
salt and pepper

To garnish
1 oz arugula
1 oz radicchio

tear the bread into bite-sized pieces and put them into a large salad bowl. Add the onion, garlic, and cucumber and stir well to mix.

whisk together the oil and vinegar, and season with salt and pepper to taste. Pour onto the salad and toss to mix. Cover and leave to stand at room temperature for at least 30 minutes.

add the tomatoes and parsley to the salad, then tear the basil leaves into the bowl. Toss to mix, then check the seasoning. Serve at room temperature, garnished with arugula and radicchio.

Serves 4
Preparation time: *20 minutes, plus standing*

clipboard: You can vary the vegetables according to what is freshest and best on the day. Peppers can be used instead of cucumber, and arugula instead of basil.

Bean and Tuna Salad

This delicious salad, which is popular all over Italy, originated in Tuscany. For a more crunchy texture, substitute a chopped raw red onion for the scallions.

16 oz can cannellini beans or
red kidney beans, drained
3 tablespoons olive oil
2 tablespoons lemon juice
3–4 scallions, chopped
7 oz can tuna, drained and broken into chunks
2 tablespoons chopped parsley
salt and pepper

To serve
Italian parsley sprigs
lemon wedges

rinse the beans thoroughly and leave in a colander to drain, then place in a salad bowl.

mix together the oil and lemon juice, and season to taste with salt and pepper. Stir the chopped scallions into the beans, pour over the dressing, and mix well.

place the tuna on top of the beans and sprinkle the chopped parsley over them. Cover with plastic wrap and refrigerate until required. Serve with Italian parsley sprigs and lemon wedges.

Serves 4
Preparation time: *15–20 minutes, plus chilling*

clipboard: This salad can be served on individual plates. Arrange some lettuce leaves on each plate, pile some of the beans in the center, and complete the salad as above.

Fried Little Pizza Pies

7 tablespoons olive oil
1 garlic clove, crushed
3 onions, sliced
1 quantity Basic Pizza Dough (see page 158)
¼ cup anchovy fillets, roughly chopped
½ cup black olives, pitted and roughly chopped
1–2 tablespoons capers, chopped
extra oil, for frying
pepper
1 quantity Tomato and Bacon Sauce (see page 79), to serve

heat 3–4 tablespoons of the olive oil in a pan and cook the garlic and onions over a gentle heat until they are soft and lightly colored.

place the dough on a lightly floured surface and work in 2 tablespoons of olive oil. Roll the dough out thinly and cut out rounds with a 3–3½-inch pastry cutter. Place a portion of the onion mixture in the center of each circle with some of the anchovies, black olives, and capers. Brush around the edge with water. Fold the dough over and press around the edge with a fork to seal well.

fry the pizzas pies in batches in shallow or deep hot fat until they are golden brown all over. Sprinkle with a little pepper just before serving and serve as hot as possible, with the tomato sauce passed separately.

Serves 4–6
Preparation time: *30–40 minutes, plus rising*
Cooking time: *4–5 minutes each batch*

clipboard: These pizza pies can also be baked in the oven. Brush them with oil on both sides and place on a baking tray, leaving room for them to rise. Leave in a warm place for about 30 minutes, then bake in a preheated oven at 450°F for 10–15 minutes until crisp and golden brown.

Spinach and Ricotta Tartlets

1 cup plain flour
¼ cup butter
2 tablespoons water

Filling
4 oz frozen chopped spinach, thawed
1 cup ricotta or curd cheese
4 teaspoons grated Parmesan cheese
2–3 pinches ground nutmeg
2 eggs, beaten
4 tablespoons light cream
salt and pepper

put the flour in a bowl with a pinch of salt. Add the butter, cut into small pieces, and rub in until the mixture resembles fine breadcrumbs. Add the water and mix to a firm dough. Turn out onto a lightly floured surface, knead briefly, then roll into a ball. Wrap in plastic wrap and refrigerate for at least 30 minutes.

divide the dough into four pieces. Roll out each piece to line a 4-inch tart pan. Place the pans on a baking tray, prick the pastry with a fork, and bake in a preheated oven at 400°F for 10 minutes.

put all the filling ingredients into a bowl and mix well. Pour into the pastry shells and return to the oven for a further 20–25 minutes until the filling has just set. Serve warm or cold with a salad.

Serves 4
Preparation time: *25 minutes, plus chilling*
Cooking time: *30–35 minutes*
Oven temperature: *400°F*

clipboard: You can double the ingredients given for the pastry and use the surplus to make a pie crust which can then be frozen for another occasion.

Fish & Shellfish

Insalata di Mare

1 pint mussels in their shells
½ cup water
8 prepared scallops, cut into pieces
12 oz monkfish, cubed
4 oz squid, cleaned and sliced
juice of 2 lemons
1 tablespoon butter
3 tablespoons finely chopped Italian parsley
12 large raw shrimp, peeled but with tails left on
2 garlic cloves, crushed
4 tablespoons olive oil
salt and pepper

soak the mussels in a bowl of cold water and discard any that are open or rise to the surface. Scrub them well to remove any barnacles, and then remove the beards.

put the mussels into a deep saucepan and add the water. Cover with a lid and cook over a high heat, shaking the pan occasionally, until the mussels open. Cook for 2 more minutes then drain and set aside to cool. Discard any mussels that do not open and remove the others from their shells.

place the scallops, monkfish, and squid on a piece of aluminum foil. Sprinkle with the juice of half a lemon, dot with butter and scatter 1 tablespoon of the parsley over the top. Fold the foil over to form a package, seal the edges, and cook in a preheated oven at 375°F for 20 minutes, or until cooked.

meanwhile put the shrimp in a baking dish and sprinkle with the garlic, the juice of half a lemon, and 1 tablespoon of the parsley. Bake, uncovered, for 10 minutes in the preheated oven. Arrange the cooked mussels, monkfish, scallops, squid, and shrimp in a serving dish and sprinkle the remaining lemon juice and the olive oil over the top. Season with salt and pepper, sprinkle with the remaining parsley, and refrigerate until required.

Serves 4–6
Preparation time: *25 minutes, plus chilling*
Cooking time: *20 minutes*
Oven temperature: *375°F*

Mixed Fried Seafood

Fritto misto mare – *mixed fried fish* – *of various sorts is found in trattorias all around the Italian coast.*

4–6 oz prepared squid, sliced
4–6 oz whitebait
4–6 oz large shrimp
4–6 oz sole fillets, skinned and cut into ½-inch strips
½ cup plain flour
vegetable oil, for deep-frying
salt and pepper
1–2 lemons, sliced or quartered, to garnish

wash all the seafood and dry thoroughly on paper towels. Season the flour well with salt and pepper.

heat the oil in a deep pan to 350–375°F, or until a cube of bread browns in 30 seconds. Toss the fish, a batch at a time, in the seasoned flour, then fry until golden brown. Drain well on paper towels, place on a warmed serving dish, and keep hot. Just before serving, sprinkle the fish lightly with salt and garnish with the lemon.

Serves 4
Preparation time: *30–40 minutes*
Cooking time: *15–20 minutes*

clipboard: Any selection of small fish or pieces of fish can be used for this dish, such as queen scallops, pieces of skate or monkfish, cooked shelled mussels, small peeled shrimp, sprats, or smelts. The quantities given are a guide only; you may prefer more or less of one type of fish.

Grilled Mussels

20 large fresh mussels
¼ cup basil leaves
I garlic clove, crushed
I small red chili, deseeded and diced
½ teaspoon grated lemon zest
I tablespoon pine nuts
I tablespoon grated Parmesan cheese
2 tablespoons fresh breadcrumbs
3–4 tablespoons extra virgin olive oil
salt and pepper

scrub the mussels well to remove any barnacles, and then remove the beards. Rinse thoroughly. Put the mussels into a large saucepan and steam them with only the water on their shells for 4 minutes until they have just opened. Discard any that do not open. Immediately plunge the mussels into cold water and drain.

lift out the mussels and carefully discard one half of each shell. Arrange the cooked mussels in their half shells in a single layer on a large dish or 4 individual gratin dishes.

combine the basil, garlic, chili, lemon zest, pine nuts, Parmesan, and half of the breadcrumbs in a food processor or blender. Process briefly to form a smooth paste and season to taste with salt and pepper. Alternatively, pound to a paste using a pestle and mortar.

transfer the basil paste to a bowl and stir in the oil. Spoon a little of the paste over each mussel and finally top each one with a few more breadcrumbs. Cook under a preheated broiler for 2–3 minutes until bubbling and golden. Serve at once.

Serves 4
Preparation time: *15 minutes*
Cooking time: *6–7 minutes*

Marinated Fried Skate

1½–2 lb skate wings, cut into pieces
½ cup white wine vinegar
½ cup olive oil
1 onion, sliced
1 bay leaf
1 thyme sprig
3 eggs, beaten
4–6 tablespoons flour
handful of Italian parsley sprigs
vegetable oil, for deep-frying
salt and pepper
1–2 lemons, sliced or quartered, to garnish

place the skate in a large pan, cover with water, and add 1 tablespoon salt. Bring to the boil and simmer gently for 10 minutes. Cool, then remove the skate from the water and drain well. Remove any thick pieces of bone and place the fish in a shallow dish.

meanwhile, make the marinade. Mix together the vinegar and olive oil with 1 teaspoon salt and ¼ teaspoon pepper. Place the onion, bay leaf, and thyme on the fish and pour over the marinade. Cover and refrigerate for 2–3 hours, turning the fish occasionally. Drain and dry the fish well.

heat the oil to 350–375°F or until a cube of bread browns in 30 seconds. Dip each piece of fish into the beaten eggs and then into the flour, and deep-fry until golden brown. Drain on paper towels and place on a warmed serving dish. Fry the parsley in the hot oil. Arrange on the dish with the fish and garnish with the lemon.

Serves 4
Preparation time: *20–30 minutes,*
  plus cooling and marinating
Cooking time: *25–30 minutes*

clipboard: In some parts of Italy, this dish is eaten cold. Instead of marinating before frying, simmer and deep-fry the fish as in the recipe then make the marinade with an extra ½ cup white wine vinegar and without the onion. Bring the marinade to the boil, pour it over the fish, then cover and refrigerate overnight or until chilled.

Pantry Shelf

Capers

Green olives

Borlotti beans

Caperberries

Black olives

Anchovies

Pesto

Tuna

Polenta

Pine nuts

Green olives

These are unripened olives, Buy them canned, bottled, in plastic bags, or by the scoop from the barrel. Green olives are also sold stuffed with anchovies, almonds, or pimientos.

Polenta

Once a peasant food, and slow and tedious to cook, this vivid yellow Italian corn meal is now available in "instant" form which cooks in 6–8 minutes. It has also made the leap to the tables of smart restaurants.

Capers

The small gray-green flower buds of a Mediterranean plant, capers are sold salted or in vinegar. Frequently used in Italian cooking, especially in sharp sauces.

Borlotti beans

These red and white speckled beans are sold dried and canned.

Caperberries

Large caper buds are sometimes sold labelled as caperberries.

Anchovies

Packed in oil or brine, anchovy fillets are an essential ingredient of many Italian dishes.

Pine nuts

Also called pine kernels, these soft little nuts are very rich and have a waxy texture. An indispensible ingredient of pesto.

Pesto

A sauce made from basil, garlic, olive oil, Parmesan cheese, and pine nuts, pesto comes from Liguria. It is delicious with pasta.

Black olives

Sold in the same ways as green olives, in their unripened form black olives have a more gentle flavour.

Tuna

Tuna responds well to the canning process. Look for

Bottled tomatoes

Balsamic vinegar

Mineral water

Olive oil

Olive oil

Artichoke hearts

Canned tomatoes

Risotto rice

Sun-dried tomatoes

Red peppers

Cannellini beans

cans containing chunks, rather than flakes, of skipjack tuna packed in oil or brine.

Bottled tomatoes and cannned tomatoes

It is impossible to imagine Italian cooking without the tomato. Canned and bottled tomatoes are available whole, chopped, and puréed (passata), with or without a flavouring of herbs.

Risotto rice

A medium-grain rice which cooks to a soft creamy texture. The best types are arborio and carnaroli rice.

Balsamic vinegar

The undisputed aristocrat of vinegars, *aceto balsamico,* from Modena in northern Italy, has an incomparable sweetness and depth not found in other vinegars.

Mineral water

Still and fizzy mineral water are an essential ingredient for every kitchen and home bar.

Olive oil

The best-known Italian olive oils come from Apulia, Tuscany, and Umbria. Look for extra virgin olive oil which is made from olives which are not subjected to any chemical treatment.

Sun-dried tomatoes

These may be sold dried, in which case they must be reconstituted, or packed in oil. They have an intense tomato flavour.

Cannellini beans

These are white kidney beans and are available both dried and canned. Like borlotti beans, they are good in salads and soups.

Red peppers

Sometimes labelled as pimientos, these peeled and deseeded red peppers are usually sold bottled but occasionally in cans.

Artichoke hearts

These can be found in canned and bottled form. They make an excellent starter when combined with a good homemade dressing.

Swordfish Palermo-style

This recipe comes from Sicily, where the swordfish are reputed to be the finest in the world.

4 swordfish steaks, about 8 oz each
flour, for dusting
½ cup olive oil
2 garlic cloves
4 anchovy fillets, finely chopped
I onion, finely chopped
4 tomatoes, skinned, deseeded and chopped
pinch of dried rosemary, crumbled
12 green olives, pitted and sliced
I tablespoon capers
salt and pepper
2 tablespoons chopped rosemary, to garnish

wash the swordfish steaks and pat them dry with paper towels. Sprinkle them with salt and dust lightly with flour on both sides.

heat the olive oil and sauté the garlic cloves over a low heat until golden. Discard the garlic and brown the swordfish steaks in the same oil, turning them once. Remove and keep warm.

add the anchovies and onion to the oil and fry until the onions are golden and the anchovies are reduced to a purée. Add the tomatoes and rosemary and simmer gently for 30 minutes, until reduced and thickened.

add the olives and capers and season to taste with salt and pepper. Return the swordfish steaks to the sauce and then heat through very gently. Serve garnished with the chopped rosemary.

Serves 4
Preparation time: *15 minutes*
Cooking time: *45 minutes*

Trota in Cartoccio

Trout is a favorite freshwater fish all over Italy.

2 tablespoons olive oil
2 garlic cloves, crushed
1 onion, chopped
1 celery stick, chopped
4 rosemary sprigs
2 tablespoons dry white wine
2 x 12 oz trout, cleaned
salt and pepper
rosemary sprigs, to garnish

heat the olive oil in a frying pan and add the garlic, onion, and celery. Sauté gently for about 5 minutes until soft and golden. Add salt and pepper, 2 of the rosemary sprigs, and the white wine. Cook gently for 5 minutes.

cut out 2 double sheets of wax paper large enough to enclose the trout. Brush the paper lightly with a little oil. Divide the sautéed onion mixture equally between the 2 pieces of paper.

wash the trout and dry well with paper towels. Sprinkle inside and out with salt and pepper. Place one trout on top of the onion mixture on each piece of paper and top with a sprig of rosemary.

fold the paper over the trout and wrap loosely, securing the sides with a double fold and double folding the ends. Place the packages on a baking sheet and cook in a preheated oven at 350°F for 20 minutes until the fish are cooked and tender. Remove the trout from the paper and serve garnished with sprigs of rosemary.

Serves 2
Preparation time: *10–15 minutes*
Cooking time: *30 minutes*
Oven temperature: *350°F*

Tonno Fresco alla Marinara

Fresh tuna in a rich sauce with tomatoes, anchovies, olives, parsley, and basil makes a splendid summer meal.

4 fresh tuna steaks, about 5 oz each
flour, for dusting
3 tablespoons olive oil
1 onion, chopped
3 garlic cloves, crushed
1½ lb tomatoes, skinned and chopped
2 tablespoons chopped Italian parsley
a few basil leaves, chopped
1 bay leaf
4 anchovy fillets, mashed
8 black olives
salt and pepper

wash the tuna steaks and pat dry with paper towels. Season with salt and plenty of pepper, then dust the steaks lightly with flour.

heat half of the olive oil in a large shallow frying pan and sauté the tuna steaks until golden on one side. Turn them and cook the other side until golden. Carefully remove them from the pan and keep them warm.

add the remaining oil to the pan and sauté the onion and garlic for about 5 minutes, until golden and soft. Add the tomatoes, parsley, basil, bay leaf, and anchovies and stir well. Bring to the boil and continue boiling until the mixture reduces and thickens slightly.

return the tuna steaks to the pan, season to taste, and simmer gently for 15 minutes, turning once. Turn off the heat, add the olives, and leave to stand for 5 minutes. Discard the bay leaf and transfer the tuna steaks in their sauce to a warmed serving dish.

Serves 4
Preparation time: *15 minutes*
Cooking time: *30 minutes*

Sole Marsala
with Parmesan cheese

The cheese and wine in this recipe make a rich, luxurious sauce for the fish. Ideally, Dover sole should be used, as it is the finest quality. Lemon sole makes a perfectly good substitute, but it will have a different flavor.

flour, for dusting
4 Dover or lemon sole, skinned
½ cup butter
2 tablespoons grated Parmesan cheese
¼ cup Fish Stock (see page 11)
3 tablespoons Marsala or dry white wine
salt and pepper
Parmesan cheese, grated, to serve

To garnish
sprigs of Italian parsley
lemon wedges

place some flour in a shallow bowl and season with salt and pepper. Dip the sole into the seasoned flour to dust them lightly on both sides. Shake off any excess flour.

heat the butter in a large frying pan. Add the floured Dover sole and cook over a gentle heat until they are golden brown on both sides, turning them once.

sprinkle the grated Parmesan over the sole and then cook very gently for another 2–3 minutes until the cheese melts.

add the fish stock and the Marsala or white wine. Cover the pan and cook over a very low heat for 4–5 minutes, until the sole are cooked and tender, and the sauce reduced. Serve sprinkled with grated Parmesan and garnish with sprigs of Italian parsley and lemon wedges.

Serves 4
Preparation time: *5 minutes*
Cooking time: *12 minutes*

Red Mullet with Tomatoes

6–8 tablespoons olive oil
1 onion, finely chopped
1 garlic clove, crushed
2–3 anchovy fillets, chopped
13 oz can chopped tomatoes
½ cup dry white wine
1 bay leaf
¼ teaspoon chopped thyme
4 tablespoons flour
4 x 6–8 oz red mullet, scales and fins removed
12 black olives, pitted
salt and pepper
thyme sprigs, to garnish

heat 2 tablespoons of the oil in a saucepan and cook the onion and garlic gently until lightly colored. Add the anchovy fillets, tomatoes, white wine, bay leaf, and thyme. Season to taste and cook gently for about 20 minutes until the sauce thickens.

meanwhile, heat 4–6 tablespoons of the oil in a frying pan. Season the flour with salt and pepper, and coat the fish with the flour. Sauté until golden brown on one side, then turn carefully and cook on the second side.

add the sauce to the pan with the red mullet and cook for a further 6–8 minutes. Transfer the fish carefully to a warmed serving dish. Toss the olives in the sauce and heat through. Remove the bay leaf and pour the sauce over the fish. Sprinkle the thyme on top and serve hot.

Serves 4
Preparation time: *15–20 minutes*
Cooking time: *30–35 minutes*

clipboard: When scraping the scales from the fish, work from the tail to the head then cut off the fins with a pair of kitchen scissors. Red mullet are usually cooked without being cleaned.

Grilled Bream
with pesto and tomato sauce

4 red bream steaks or fillets, about 6 oz each
6 tablespoons olive oil
4 large tomatoes, skinned, deseeded and chopped
4 anchovy fillets, chopped
3 tablespoons Pesto (see page 80)
salt and pepper

To serve
basil sprigs
green salad
crusty bread

season the bream steaks on both sides with salt and pepper, and brush with 2 tablespoons of the olive oil.

cook under a preheated broiler for 4–5 minutes on each side. Alternatively, cook the bream on the greased grill of a preheated barbecue, putting the fish on a special grid if the bars of the barbecue are very wide apart.

meanwhile make the sauce. Heat the remaining 4 tablespoons of olive oil in a pan. Add the tomatoes and anchovy fillets, and salt and pepper to taste (remember that anchovies are very salty). Cook gently for 5 minutes.

stir the pesto sauce into the tomato and anchovy mixture.

put the bream steaks on to a warmed serving dish and spoon over the sauce. Garnish with basil sprigs and serve with a green salad and lots of crusty bread.

Serves 4
Preparation time: *4–5 minutes*
Cooking time: *about 10 minutes*

Octopus and Tomato Salad

Nothing impresses more than tentacles from the sea.

4 tablespoons soy sauce
4 tablespoons Italian salad dressing (see below)
¼ cup soft brown sugar
2 lb small octopus, cleaned
3 tablespoons olive oil, plus extra for brushing
1 lb ripe plum tomatoes, cut in half lengthways
1 teaspoon sea salt

Italian salad dressing
4–6 tablespoons olive oil
2 tablespoons red or white vinegar
1 garlic clove, crushed
salt and pepper

To garnish
dill sprigs
lime wedges

combine the soy sauce, Italian salad dressing, and brown sugar in a bowl. Add the octopus and mix to coat. Cover and refrigerate for 1 hour.

brush a baking sheet with olive oil. Place the tomatoes, cut-side up, on the sheet and sprinkle with sea salt. Drizzle 1 tablespoon of the olive oil over the tomatoes and bake in a preheated oven at 400°F for about 10 minutes.

heat the remaining oil in a large frying pan. Drain the octopus and add to the frying pan. Cook the octopus in batches, turning often, on a high heat for 1–2 minutes until just tender but cooked.

serve the octopus in a large bowl with the roasted tomatoes. Garnish the dish with dill sprigs and lime wedges.

Serves 6
Preparation time: *20 minutes, plus marinating*
Cooking time: *about 12 minutes*
Oven temperature: *400°F*

Pasta & Gnocchi

Fresh Pasta

is quite simple to make at home

3 cups all-purpose flour, sifted
pinch of salt
3 eggs
1 tablespoon olive oil
flour, for dusting

place the flour and a pinch of salt on a work surface. Make a well in the center and add the eggs. Using your fingertips, draw the flour in from the sides and mix well. Add the olive oil and continue mixing until you have a soft dough. Alternatively, make the dough in a food processor.

turn out the dough onto a lightly floured surface and knead well until it is really smooth and silky. Roll out the dough, giving it an occasional quarter-turn and stretching it out, until it resembles a thin sheet of cloth and is almost transparent.

hang the pasta over the back of a chair, a broom handle, or a pasta stand and leave for about 10 minutes to dry. Alternatively, lay it on a table with one-third overhanging the edge and keep turning it so that it dries out completely.

roll up the pasta loosely like a jelly roll and then cut through horizontally at regular intervals to make fettuccine (⅛ inch wide) or tagliatelle (¼ inch wide). Unravel them and toss gently in a little flour. Leave them to dry on a cloth for at least 30 minutes then cook in a large pan of lightly salted boiling water, until tender but firm to the bite. Serve tossed with olive oil, garlic, salt and pepper, and parsley, or with the pasta sauce of your choice.

Serves 4
Preparation time: *1 hour*
Cooking time: *2–3 minutes*

clipboard: To make lasagne or ravioli, cut the pasta into sheets rather than strips.

Tagliatelle al Sugo di Pomodoro

12 oz dried tagliatelle
1 teaspoon vegetable oil
1 tablespoon olive oil
Parmesan cheese shavings, to serve

Tomato Sauce
3 tablespoons olive oil
2 onions, chopped
2 garlic cloves, crushed
1 lb plum tomatoes, skinned and chopped
2 tablespoons tomato purée
1 teaspoon sugar
½ cup dry white wine
few ripe olives, pitted and quartered
2–3 tablespoons torn basil leaves
salt and pepper

first make the tomato sauce. Heat the olive oil in a large frying pan. Add the onions and garlic, and sauté gently over a low heat until they are tender and lightly colored, stirring the mixture occasionally.

add the tomatoes and tomato purée together with the sugar and wine, stirring well. Cook over a low heat until the mixture is quite thick and reduced. Stir in the olives and basil leaves and season to taste with salt and plenty of pepper.

meanwhile, cook the tagliatelle with the vegetable oil in a large pan of boiling salted water, until the pasta is tender but firm to the bite.

drain the tagliatelle immediately, mixing in the olive oil and seasoning well with pepper. Arrange the pasta on 4 warmed serving plates and top with the tomato sauce, stirring it into the tagliatelle. Serve sprinkled with Parmesan shavings.

Serves 4
Preparation time: *10 minutes*
Cooking time: *20 minutes*

Fusilli with Eggplant
and tomato and bacon sauce

1 large eggplant, diced
½ cup olive oil
1 lb dried fusilli
1 quantity Tomato and Bacon Sauce (see clipboard, below)
salt and pepper
basil sprigs and leaves, to serve

put the eggplant into a colander and sprinkle with salt. Leave for at least 30 minutes to drain. This will remove some of the bitter juices from the eggplant. Rinse thoroughly, drain well, and dry on paper towels.

heat half of the oil in a frying pan and cook some of the eggplant dice until golden brown. Repeat, adding more oil to the pan if necessary until all the eggplant is cooked. Keep hot.

cook the fusilli in a large pan of boiling lightly salted water for about 12 minutes, until tender but firm to the bite. Drain well and stir into the hot sauce. Check the seasoning and add salt and pepper to taste. Turn into a serving bowl and put the fried eggplant on top. Serve sprinkled with basil sprigs and leaves.

Serves 4
Preparation time: *20 minutes, plus draining*
Cooking time: *40–45 minutes*

clipboard: To make the Tomato and Bacon Sauce, gently fry 1 chopped onion, 2 crushed garlic cloves, and 2 slices of bacon in 1–2 tablespoons of olive oil. When soft, add a 13 oz can chopped tomatoes, and season with salt and pepper. Simmer for 25–30 minutes until thickened. For a smooth sauce, liquidize, then sieve to remove the seeds.

Tagliatelle al Pesto

1 lb tagliatelle
salt and pepper
½ cup grated Parmesan cheese, to serve

Pesto
½ cup pine nuts
1 garlic clove, crushed
½ cup basil leaves
¾ cup grated Parmesan cheese
juice of ½ lemon
½ cup olive oil

to make the pesto, spread the pine nuts on a baking sheet and place in a preheated oven at 425°F for 3–5 minutes, until golden. Keep checking them to make sure that they do not burn.

pound the pine nuts with the garlic to a thick paste using a pestle and mortar. Alternatively, use a food processor or blender.

tear the basil leaves into shreds and add to the pine nut mixture. Continue pounding or processing until you have a thick green paste. Transfer to a bowl (if using a mortar) and stir in the grated Parmesan and lemon juice. Add the olive oil, a little at a time, beating well in between each addition.

cook the tagliatelle in a large pan of boiling salted water, until tender but firm to the bite; drain well. Sprinkle with pepper and toss the pasta lightly with the pesto sauce. Serve sprinkled with Parmesan.

Serves 4
Preparation time: *15–20 minutes*
Cooking time: *5–12 minutes*
Oven temperature: *425°F*

Fusilli with Anchovies and Olives

1 teaspoon vegetable oil
12 oz dried fusilli
2 tablespoons butter
6 anchovy fillets, chopped
1 tablespoon tomato purée
1 tablespoon olive paste
6 pitted black olives, chopped
handful of basil leaves
salt and pepper
grated Parmesan cheese, to garnish

bring a large pan of salted water to a boil. Add the oil. Cook the pasta for 8–12 minutes or according to package instructions, until just tender but firm to the bite.

drain the pasta and set it aside. Melt the butter in a large saucepan. Add the anchovy fillets, tomato purée, olive paste, and olives. Stir over the heat until the mixture sizzles. Season well with pepper. Cool for 1 minute.

add the drained pasta to the saucepan and toss well. Tear the basil leaves into pieces and add them to the pasta. Serve immediately, garnished with grated Parmesan.

Serves 4
Preparation time: *10 minutes*
Cooking time: *about 15 minutes*

Spaghetti alla Bolognese

This is one of countless meat and vegetable sauces that are served with pasta. The beautiful city of Bologna, which gives this recipe its name, is renowned for its fine pasta and is the home of several classic Italian recipes.

1 lb spaghetti
1 teaspoon olive oil
pepper
½ cup Parmesan cheese, to serve

Meat Sauce
4 tablespoons olive oil
1 onion, finely chopped
1 garlic clove, crushed
4 slices of bacon, chopped
1 carrot, diced
1 celery stick, diced
1 lb lean ground beef
½ cup red wine
½ cup milk
grated nutmeg
13 oz can chopped tomatoes
1 tablespoon sugar
1 teaspoon chopped oregano
salt and pepper

first make the meat sauce. Heat the oil in a saucepan or deep frying pan and sauté the onion, garlic, bacon, carrot, and celery until soft and golden. Add the beef and cook, stirring occasionally, until browned. Add the red wine and bring to a boil. Reduce the heat slightly and cook over a moderate heat until most of the wine has evaporated. Season with salt and pepper.

add the milk and a little grated nutmeg, and stir well. Continue cooking until the milk has been absorbed by the meat mixture. Add the tomatoes, sugar, and oregano. Reduce the heat to a gentle simmer and cook, uncovered, for at least 1 hour, stirring occasionally, until the sauce is reduced and richly colored.

cook the spaghetti with the olive oil in a large pan of lightly salted boiling water until tender but firm to the bite. Drain well and season with pepper. Pour the meat sauce over the spaghetti and serve the Parmesan separately.

Serves 4
Preparation time: *15 minutes*
Cooking time: *about 1½ hours*

Conchiglie with Calabrian Sauce

20 oz can tomatoes

olive oil, for frying

2 garlic cloves, each cut into 3–4 pieces

1 chili, cored and deseeded

4 oz salami, thickly sliced

1 lb conchiglie

salt

3 oz pecorino cheese shavings, to serve

crush the tomatoes or purée them briefly in a food processor. Coat the bottom of a saucepan with olive oil. Add the garlic and chili and sauté gently until the garlic is golden, crushing the chili against the bottom of the pan to release its flavor. Add the tomatoes and the slices of salami, with salt to taste. Simmer gently for about 30 minutes, until the sauce becomes denser and darker in color.

meanwhile cook the conchiglie in boiling salted water according to package instructions, until just tender but firm to the bite. Drain, transfer to a warmed serving dish, and pour the sauce over the top. Serve with the pecorino shavings.

Serves 4
Preparation time: *15 minutes*
Cooking time: *about 35 minutes*

clipboard: In Calabria this dish is served with grated ricotta which has been left to mature and is no longer a fresh curd cheese.

Fresh & Dry Pasta

Fusilli verdi

Conchiglie

Tortellini

Farfalle

Assorted fiorelli

Fusilli verdi
Fusilli means twists or corkscrews. Because they are virtually made of ridges, fusilli are one of the shapes that hold a lot of sauce. They are shown above coloured green with spinach. Water can be held in the fusilli ridges so extra care is needed when draining them.

Conchiglie
These are shell-shaped pasta – their name translates as little shells or conches. They come in various sizes and may have a smooth surface or a ribbed texture (*rigate*), as shown here. Conchiglie go well with minced meat sauces. As with fusilli, special care is needed when draining them.

Tortellini
Tortellini are a small version of tortelli, a stuffed pasta shape which originated in Bologna. Spinach and ricotta is a favorite filling for tortellini; they are sold ready-filled or you can make your own. Like ravioli, they are served with a sauce or with melted butter and grated Parmesan.

Farfalle
The name of this small shape translates as bows or butterflies, and it is available in a variety of sizes. Fresh and dried farfalle, and other pastas, have a different cooking time, and pasta produced by different manufacturers can also vary, so always read the package instructions carefully before starting to cook.

Assorted fiorelli
The name of this pretty little pasta shape means flower. It is sold in packets of mixed colors – white, green, and red – the Italian national colors. Green pasta is colored with spinach, red with tomatoes. Also available, but not so easy to find, are black, colored with squid ink, and brown, with mushrooms.

Spaghetti

Fresh tagliatelle

Lasagne verdi

Penne

Pappardelle

Spaghetti

The classic pasta, and possibly the universal favorite, spaghetti may be fresh or dried, the dried form including a wholemeal version. Other long strings or ribbons of pasta include *tagliatelle*, *spaghettini* (a very thin type of spaghetti), *fusilli lunghi* (an elongated corkscrew shape), *taglionini* and *fettuccine*.

Penne

The name of this short tubular-shaped pasta means quills, recalling the quill pens of olden times. Penne may be smooth or with a ridged surface. Among the many other small pasta shapes are *lumache* (snail shells), *ditali* (thimbles), *orecciette* (ears), *ruoti* (wheels), and *capelleti* (little hats).

Tagliatelle

The fresh egg tagliatelle shown above is coiled into nests. Tagliatelle, which came originally from Bologna, is a flat ribbon pasta and so technically a noodle. The combination of green and yellow tagliatelle is known as *paglio e fieno* or hay and straw noodles. It is also available dried.

Pappardelle

This is a wide ribbon noodle, sometimes made even more distinctive by a crinkly edge. Like tagliatelle, it can be found coiled into nests.

Lasagne verdi

Lasagne is made in broad flat sheets which may be fresh or dried. The sheets are usually cooked layered with meat, cheese, vegetables, and a sauce, or sauces, and baked in the oven. A dish made with a combination of plain and green lasagne can look very effective. Cannelloni are sometimes made with sheets of lasagne.

Spaghetti alla Vongole

7 cups fresh clams
½ cup dry white wine
2 tablespoons olive oil
3 garlic cloves, finely chopped
1½ lb tomatoes, skinned and chopped
1 lb spaghetti or spaghettini
1 teaspoon vegetable oil
2 tablespoons chopped Italian parsley
salt and pepper

scrub the clams under cold running water to remove all sand and grit. Discard any that do not close when tapped. Put the clams into a saucepan, add the wine, cover, and cook for 5 minutes. Strain, reserving the liquid. Remove the clams from their shells, discarding any that have not opened, and leaving a few in their half shells for garnish.

heat the oil in a saucepan and sauté the garlic until just golden. Add the tomatoes and simmer gently for 10 minutes.

cook the spaghetti with the vegetable oil in a large pan of boiling lightly salted water for 8–12 minutes, or according to the package instructions, until tender but firm to the bite.

meanwhile add the clams, the strained cooking liquid, and parsley to the tomato mixture and season to taste. Cook gently for 5 minutes to heat through. Drain the pasta thoroughly and mix with the sauce over a gentle heat. Transfer to a warmed serving dish and serve immediately.

Serves 4–6
Preparation time: *20 minutes*
Cooking time: *25–30 minutes*

Cannelloni

In Italian the word cannelloni means "big pipes" – an appropriate description for these filled pasta tubes.

8 pieces wide dried lasagne
1 teaspoon vegetable oil
¼ cup grated Parmesan cheese
1 tablespoon butter

Filling

2 tablespoons olive oil
½ cup chopped onions
1 garlic clove, crushed
½ lb finely ground beef
2 tomatoes, skinned, deseeded, and chopped
1 tablespoon fine breadcrumbs
¼ cup grated Parmesan cheese
¼ teaspoon dried marjoram
1 egg, lightly beaten
salt and pepper

Sauce

3 tablespoons butter
3 tablespoons flour
1 cup hot milk
1 cup hot light cream
grated nutmeg
salt and pepper

first make the filling. Heat the oil in a saucepan, add the onions and garlic and sauté for 5 minutes until soft. Add the ground beef and cook, stirring, until browned. Add the tomatoes, cover, and cook for 10 minutes over a low heat. Remove the pan from the heat and stir in the breadcrumbs, Parmesan, marjoram, egg, and salt and pepper to taste. Set aside to cool.

to make the sauce, melt the butter in a saucepan and stir in the flour. Cook gently over a low heat for 1 minute, stirring well. Remove from the heat and whisk in the milk and cream. Return to the heat and bring to a boil, whisking all the time, until thick and smooth. Season with salt, pepper, and nutmeg to taste. Cover and keep warm.

cook the lasagne with the oil in a large pan of boiling lightly salted water for a few minutes, according to the package instructions, until tender but firm to the bite. Remove with a slotted spoon and drain well.

spoon a little of the filling down one long side of each sheet of lasagne. Roll up each one into a cylinder. Arrange the cylinders side by side in a well-buttered ovenproof dish. Spoon the sauce over the top to cover the pasta completely. Sprinkle with the Parmesan, dot with butter and bake in a preheated oven at 375°F for 20–30 minutes until bubbling and golden.

Serves 4
Preparation time: *15 minutes*
Cooking time: *about 1 hour*
Oven temperature: *375°F*

Cannelloni *with spinach*

1½ lb fresh spinach, stalks removed
4 tablespoons butter
1 cup ricotta or cottage cheese, sieved
¾ cup grated Parmesan cheese
pinch of grated nutmeg
2 large eggs
12 large cannelloni tubes
1 teaspoon olive oil
1 tablespoon flour
1 cup milk
4 tablespoons bran cereal
salt and pepper

wash the spinach, place it in a large saucepan with just the water that clings to the leaves, and heat gently for 3–4 minutes until wilted. Drain in a colander, pressing out all the moisture, then chop finely.

melt half of the butter in a saucepan, add the spinach and stir well. Remove from the heat. Beat the ricotta or cottage cheese and half of the Parmesan into the spinach and season with salt, pepper, and nutmeg. Beat in the eggs. Set aside to cool.

cook the cannelloni tubes in plenty of boiling salted water with the oil for about 10 minutes, or according to the package instructions, until they are just tender but firm to the bite. Drain, refresh in cold water, and drain again. Dry thoroughly with paper towels. Set aside to cool.

melt the remaining butter in a pan, stir in the flour and cook for 1 minute. Remove from the heat and gradually stir in the milk, stirring constantly. Bring to the boil, season with salt and pepper, and simmer for 5 minutes. Taste and adjust the seasoning if necessary.

spoon the spinach filling into the cannelloni tubes with a teaspoon and place them in a greased, shallow baking dish. Pour the sauce over the top and sprinkle with the remaining Parmesan mixed with the bran cereal.

bake in a preheated oven at 350°F for 35–40 minutes or until the topping is brown and crusty.

Serves 4–6
Preparation time: *20 minutes, plus cooling*
Cooking time: *45 minutes–1 hour*
Oven temperature: *350°F*

Lasagne al Forno

This is the classic version of lasagne — from Emilia Romagna in northern Italy — sheets of pasta layered with a meat sauce and a bechamel sauce, sprinkled with freshly grated Parmesan and baked in the oven.

1 quantity Meat Sauce (see page 84)
8 oz dried lasagne
1 teaspoon vegetable oil
½ cup grated Parmesan cheese
1 tablespoon butter
mixed green salad, to serve

Bechamel Sauce
2 tablespoons butter
2 tablespoons flour
2 cups milk
pinch of ground nutmeg
salt and pepper

simmer the meat sauce gently for at least 1 hour.

meanwhile, make the bechamel sauce. Melt the butter in a saucepan and stir in the flour. Cook over gentle heat, without browning, for 2–3 minutes, and then gradually beat in the milk until the sauce is thick, smooth, and glossy. Season with salt, pepper, and nutmeg, and cook gently for 5–10 minutes.

cook the lasagne with the vegetable oil in a large pan of boiling lightly salted water according to the package instructions, until just tender but firm to the bite. Drain and pat dry. Put a little of the meat sauce in a buttered ovenproof dish and cover with a layer of lasagne and then another layer of meat sauce topped with some white sauce. Continue layering in this way, ending with a layer of lasagne and a topping of white sauce.

sprinkle with the grated Parmesan and then dot the top with butter. Bake in a preheated oven at 450°F for 30 minutes until the lasagne is golden brown. Serve hot with a green salad.

Serves 4
Preparation time: *30 minutes*
Cooking time: *1¾ hours*
Oven temperature: *450°F*

Mushroom and Mozzarella Lasagne Stacks

2 tablespoons olive oil
4 tablespoons butter
2 onions, chopped
2 garlic cloves, chopped
1 lb mushrooms, trimmed and sliced
4 tablespoons heavy cream
4 tablespoons dry white wine
1 teaspoon chopped thyme
8 pieces dried lasagne
1 tablespoon vegetable oil
2 red bell peppers, skinned (see page 30) cored, deseeded, and thickly sliced
¼ lb young spinach leaves
¼ lb mozzarella cheese
salt and pepper
Parmesan cheese shavings

heat the oil and butter in a saucepan, add the onions and sauté for 3 minutes. Add the garlic and cook for 1 minute.

add the mushrooms, turn up the heat and cook for 5 minutes. Add the cream, white wine, and thyme, season with salt and pepper and simmer for 4 minutes.

bring a pan of water to the boil, add the lasagne sheets a few pieces at a time and the vegetable oil, and cook for 7 minutes or according to the package instructions, until tender but firm to the bite. Remove from the pan and place 4 pieces in a well-oiled large ovenproof dish.

place a generous spoonful of mushroom mixture on each piece of lasagne, add some red pepper slices and half of the spinach and place another piece of lasagne on top. Then add the remaining spinach, a little more mushroom mixture, and top with a slice of mozzarella. Finish with the Parmesan shavings. Place the dish under a preheated very hot broiler and cook for 5 minutes until the Parmesan is bubbling.

Serves 4
Preparation time: *10 minutes*
Cooking time: *20 minutes*

Ravioli di Spinaci e Ricotta

1 quantity Fresh Pasta Dough (see page 74)

Filling

8 oz spinach
½ cup fresh ricotta cheese
¼ cup grated Parmesan cheese
grated nutmeg
1 egg, beaten
salt and pepper

To serve

4 tablespoons butter, melted
3–4 sage leaves, torn
Parmesan cheese, grated

first make the filling. Wash the spinach, place it in a saucepan with just the water that clings to the leaves and heat gently for 3–4 minutes until wilted. Drain the spinach in a colander, pressing out all the moisture, then chop it roughly.

place the ricotta and Parmesan in a bowl and mix in the chopped spinach. Add the grated nutmeg and beaten egg, season with salt and pepper, and mix well to a paste.

roll out the pasta as thinly as possible on a lightly floured surface and cut into 2 equal pieces. Place teaspoons of the ricotta and spinach filling over one piece of pasta at regular intervals, about 2 inches apart.

cover with the other sheet of pasta and press gently around each little mound with your fingers. Using a pastry cutter wheel, cut the pasta into squares, each containing a mound of filling. Cook the ravioli in a large pan of gently boiling water for 4–5 minutes, until they rise to the surface. Drain and serve with melted butter, garnished with sage and Parmesan.

Serves 4–6
Preparation time: *25 minutes*
Cooking time: *10 minutes*

Spinach and Ricotta Gnocchi

These delicate gnocchi are piped straight into a pan of boiling water, making them quicker and easier to prepare than potato gnocchi.

4 oz frozen spinach, thawed
1 cup ricotta cheese
2 small eggs, beaten
4 tablespoons grated Parmesan cheese
1 tablespoon chopped basil
4 tablespoons flour
salt and pepper
Parmesan cheese, grated, to serve

Sauce
4 tablespoons unsalted butter
1 garlic clove, crushed
1 red chili, deseeded and chopped

squeeze out the excess water from the spinach and chop finely. Place in a food processor or blender with the ricotta and process until smooth. Beat in the eggs, basil, Parmesan, and salt and pepper to taste, and enough flour to form a soft, slightly sticky dough.

bring a large pan of salted water to the boil. Transfer the spinach mixture to a piping bag fitted with a large plain nozzle. As soon as the water is boiling, pipe about 12 short lengths of gnocchi into the water, using a sharp knife to cut away from the nozzle as you pipe.

cook the gnocchi for 2–3 minutes until they rise to the surface, then remove with a slotted spoon, drain on paper towels, and transfer to a warmed serving dish. Keep warm while cooking the remaining gnocchi.

to make the sauce, melt the butter in a small pan and sauté the garlic and chili for 2 minutes. Pour over the gnocchi and toss well. Sprinkle with Parmesan and serve at once.

Serves 4
Preparation time: *20 minutes*
Cooking time: *12–15 minutes*

Beef, Lamb, & Pork

Leg of Lamb Roman-style

2–3 lb leg of lamb
3 garlic cloves, peeled
2–3 rosemary sprigs, chopped
7 tablespoons olive oil
2 canned anchovies, soaked in milk and drained
3–4 tablespoons wine vinegar
salt and pepper

make small incisions in the lamb and insert a slice of garlic and a few rosemary leaves into each one.

heat half of the oil in a large flameproof casserole, add 1 garlic clove, and fry until browned. Remove the garlic, then add the leg of lamb to the casserole. Sauté the meat over a moderate heat, turning until browned on all sides. Sprinkle with salt and pepper to taste. Cover and cook in a preheated oven at 375°F for 1½ hours or until tender, basting and turning frequently.

pound the rosemary, the remaining garlic, and the anchovies using a pestle and mortar, then stir in the remaining oil and the vinegar. Transfer the lamb to a warmed serving dish. Add the rosemary mixture to the casserole and simmer until reduced. Pour the juices over the lamb and serve immediately.

Serves 4
Preparation time: *15 minutes*
Cooking time: *about 1¾ hours*
Oven temperature: *375°F*

clipboard: Anchovies can be very salty. Soaking them in milk for about 15 minutes or so before cooking will remove some of their saltiness.

Salumeria

Fresh sausages

Salami felinetto

Calabrese salami

Salami felinetto

There are said to be almost as many different types of salami as there are towns and villages in Italy. They are all a tightly packed meat mixture, usually of pork and pork fat but sometimes with beef, veal, and wild boar, and with a variety of flavorings. *Salami felinetto*, see above, describes a hard salami.

Fresh sausages

Fresh Italian pork sausages – *salsiccia puro suino* – may be mild, herby, or hot and spicy in flavor, but they always have a high meat content. Salamelle is a fresh sausage sold in links and *salsiccie a metro* is a long sausage that gets it name because it was traditionally sold by length, although nowadays it is sold by weight.

Calabrese salami

This is one of the harder salamis and comes from Calabria in southern Italy. It is flavored with a spicy mixture of paprika, peppercorns, and chillies and, like all salamis, it has excellent keeping qualities.

Proscuitto di Parma

This is also known as Parma ham. When the Italians refer to proscuitto they always mean *proscuitto crudo* or raw ham. (*Proscuitto cotto* is boiled or baked ham.) Parma ham is pink in color and marbled with white fat; it is most often served as an antipasto, in thin slices and with sliced melon or figs.

Bresaolo

This high quality salted raw beef is a speciality of Lombardy. It is extremely expensive, the result of its lengthy curing process. Served in thin slices, it makes a delicious starter when served with a simple dressing of olive oil, lemon juice, finely chopped parsley, and pepper.

Bresaolo

Salami Milanese

Mortadella

Pancetta

…cuitto di Parma

Salami Napoli

Bocconcino

Salami Milanese

This is one the best known Italian salamis and exported widely all over the world. It is also known as *crespone* and is a finely minced pork salami flavored with garlic which has been crushed in red wine.

Salami Napoli

Another well-known and widely available sausage, Neapolitan salami is made with a combination of pork, beef, and pork fat. A coarsely ground salami, it is generously spiced with chili and garlic.

Mortadella

The best known of all the Italian slicing sausages, mortadella is a large lightly smoked sausage made of finely minced pork or a mixture of meats. It is seasoned with parsley and studded with olives, pistachio nuts, and small cubes of fat.

Bocconcino

These are small, sausage-shaped salamis which are sold in a string. They are made of raw pork or other red meat interspersed with fat and are very highly seasoned. Bocconcino should be sliced finely and eaten in salads or in sandwiches.

Pancetta

This is unsmoked bacon taken from the belly of the pig. It is cured with spices, salt, and pepper. The bacon is then rolled into a sausage shape and sliced very thinly. Pancetta is also diced and used as a flavoring in soups and stews.

Calves' Liver Venetian-style

6 tablespoons olive oil
1 tablespoon butter
4 onions, thinly sliced
1¼ lb calves' liver, thinly sliced
4 tablespoons Chicken Stock (see page 10)
1 tablespoon wine vinegar
2 tablespoons finely chopped parsley
salt and pepper

heat the olive oil with the butter in a large heavy frying pan. Add the onions and cook gently over a very low heat, stirring occasionally, for about 40 minutes, or until the onions are soft, golden, and translucent but not browned. Remove the onions with a slotted spoon and keep warm.

add the thinly sliced calves' liver to the pan and sauté very quickly until brown on one side. Turn over and quickly cook the other side. The liver should be lightly browned on the outside and still pink in the middle. Remove and keep warm.

add the chicken stock and vinegar to the pan and bring to a boil, scraping the bottom of the pan with a wooden spoon to pick up the juices from the liver and stirring until the sauce reduces. Season to taste with salt and pepper, and stir in the chopped parsley.

arrange the liver and onions on a heated serving dish or four warmed serving plates, and pour the sauce over the top. Serve with a bowl of fresh pasta and a crisp green salad.

Serves 4
Preparation time: *10 minutes*
Cooking time: *1¼ hours*

La Fiorentina

This must be one of Tuscany's most famous dishes. It is unbelievably simple to make, but it does need good quality steak. In this recipe a thick cut of sirloin is used instead of the usual T-bone. Here it is cooked on a barbecue, but broil if you prefer.

1 sirloin steak, 1–1½ inches thick
about 2 tablespoons olive oil
salt and pepper
salad leaves, to serve

prepare the barbecue and let it burn until all the flames have died down and the coals have turned grey.

put the steak on the barbecue grill and cook for 5 minutes, then turn the steak over and sprinkle the cooked side with salt and pepper. Cook for a further 5 minutes, turn again, and sprinkle the second cooked side with salt and pepper. Cook for 2 minutes.

remove the steak from the barbecue grill and sprinkle with olive oil. Serve immediately with salad leaves.

Serves 1
Preparation time: *1–2 minutes, plus preparing the barbecue*
Cooking time: *12 minutes*

clipboard: *La Fiorentina* is traditionally served very rare, and the cooking time given here is for rare steak, but you can cook the meat longer if you prefer.

Beef Steaks Pizzaiolo

6 tablespoons olive oil
1–2 garlic cloves, crushed
1 lb tomatoes, skinned and chopped, or
13 oz can chopped tomatoes
1 teaspoon chopped oregano
4 x 8 oz thinly cut steak, trimmed of
all fat
salt and pepper
oregano sprigs, to garnish

heat three-quarters of the oil in a saucepan and cook the garlic gently until golden brown. Add the tomatoes, season lightly with salt and pepper, and add the oregano. Bring to a boil and simmer for 10–15 minutes, until the sauce thickens slightly.

meanwhile heat the remaining oil in a frying pan and quickly brown the meat on both sides. Pour the tomato sauce over the meat and continue cooking very gently for 10–15 minutes, or until the meat is tender. If necessary, add a little water to prevent the sauce reducing too much.

arrange the steaks on warmed individual plates or a serving dish and pour over the sauce. Garnish with oregano sprigs and serve immediately.

Serves 4
Preparation time: *15–20 minutes*
Cooking time: *25–35 minutes*

clipboard: This dish gets its name because it is cooked like a pizza with a topping of tomatoes, garlic, and oregano. It is a very good recipe to use for steaks which are not very tender, or with pork chops. Simmer very gently until they tenderize, taking care that the sauce never boils as this would toughen the meat.

Stuffed Beef Olives

2 lb rump steak or round steak
½ cup grated pecorino cheese
2 slices Parma ham, chopped
3 garlic cloves, crushed
3 tablespoons chopped Italian parsley
I tablespoon chopped basil
3 tablespoons olive oil
salt and pepper
few basil leaves, to garnish

Tomato Sauce
I onion, chopped
2 garlic cloves, crushed
2 lb tomatoes, skinned and chopped
I tablespoon tomato purée
½ cup red wine

cut the beef steaks into thin slices and place between 2 sheets of wax paper. Flatten them with a rolling pin and then season on both sides with salt and pepper.

to make the filling, place the grated pecorino in a bowl with the chopped ham, garlic, parsley, and basil. Mix well together and spread a little of this mixture on to each slice of beef. Roll up, folding in the sides, and secure with fine string.

heat the olive oil in a large saucepan and gently sauté the beef olives until they are lightly browned all over, turning as necessary. Remove from the pan and keep warm.

to make the sauce, add the onion and garlic to the oil in the pan and sauté until soft. Add the tomatoes, tomato purée, wine, and salt and pepper to taste. Bring to a boil, and then add the beef olives. Cover and simmer gently for 1½–2 hours, or until tender. Remove the string from the beef olives and serve with the sauce, sprinkled with basil.

Serves 6
Preparation time: *20 minutes*
Cooking time: *1¾–2¼ hours*

Pork, Ham, and Sage Rolls

¼ cup white sultanas

4 tablespoons Marsala

4 long thin pork steaks (cut from the tenderloin), about 3 oz each

4 thick slices Parma ham

1 tablespoon chopped sage

16 cubes white bread, about 1 inch square

4 tablespoons olive oil

8 thin slices bacon, cut in half

salt and pepper

mix the sultanas with the Marsala. Cover and leave to stand for 1 hour.

cut each pork steak into 4 long strips, then cut the slices of ham into strips roughly the same size.

lay a strip of ham on top of each strip of pork. Sprinkle each strip with some chopped sage, a few of the sultanas, and salt and pepper to taste. Roll each strip up neatly, so that you have 16 sausage shapes.

brush each cube of bread with a little olive oil, then roll each one in half a bacon slice.

thread 4 pork and ham rolls and 4 bread and bacon rolls alternately on to each of four kebab skewers. Brush the kebabs with olive oil.

cook on the oiled grill of a preheated barbecue or under a preheated broiler for 3–4 minutes on each side. Serve hot with a green salad.

Serves 4
Preparation time: *30 minutes, plus standing*
Cooking time: *7–8 minutes*

Sausages

with beans and sage

*Ask at your Italian delicatessen for fresh pork sausages —
salsiccia puro suino. There are many different kinds but
whichever you choose, they are bound to have a high meat
content because this is how Italians like their sausages.*

8 oz dried cannellini beans, soaked overnight
5 tablespoons olive oil
1 lb Italian pork sausages, chopped
8 fl oz passata (Italian puréed tomatoes)
2 garlic cloves, crushed
1 sage sprig
salt and pepper
sage leaves, to garnish

drain the beans and rinse under cold running water. Place them in a large saucepan, cover with water, and bring to a boil. Boil rapidly for 10 minutes, then lower the heat and half cover with a lid. Simmer for 1¼ hours or until the beans are tender, skimming off the scum and adding water as necessary. Drain the beans and reserve the cooking liquid.

heat 3 tablespoons of the oil in a large flameproof casserole, add the sausages, and cook over a moderate heat until browned on all sides. Add the passata, garlic, sage, and salt and pepper to taste and stir well to mix. Bring to the boil, then add the beans and a few spoonfuls of the cooking liquid. Cover and simmer, stirring frequently, for 15 minutes — the consistency should be quite thick. Taste for seasoning.

drizzle the remaining olive oil over the dish and serve garnished with fresh sage leaves.

Serves 4
Preparation time: *15 minutes,
 plus soaking*
Cooking time: *about 1¾ hours*

Veal Chops with Gremolata

6 tablespoons flour
4 thin veal chops
4 tablespoons butter
1 tablespoon olive oil
2 onions, chopped
2 garlic cloves, crushed and chopped
2 celery sticks, chopped
1 carrot, chopped
2 bay leaves
6 tomatoes, skinned, deseeded, and chopped
½ cup Chicken Stock (see page 10)
½ cup dry white wine
salt and pepper

Gremolata
2 tablespoons finely chopped Italian parsley
1 tablespoon finely chopped sage
finely grated zest of 3 lemons
3 large garlic cloves, chopped

season the flour with salt and pepper and coat both sides of the veal chops. Melt the butter and oil in a large flameproof casserole, add the chops, and brown well on each side. Remove the chops from the casserole and keep them warm.

add the onions, garlic, celery, and carrot to the casserole and sauté, stirring, for 3 minutes.

add the bay leaves, tomatoes, stock, wine, and salt and pepper, mix well and bring to a boil. Return the chops to the casserole and turn to coat them thoroughly in the sauce. Cover and cook in a preheated oven at 400°F for 20 minutes.

meanwhile, make the gremolata. Mix together the parsley, sage, lemon zest, and garlic.

transfer the chops to a warmed serving platter and keep them warm. Boil the sauce to reduce if necessary, remove the bay leaves, then pour the sauce over the chops. Spoon some of the gremolata over each one and serve.

Serves 4
Preparation time: *10 minutes*
Cooking time: *35 minutes*
Oven temperature: *400°F*

Veal Olives with Mushrooms

12 small veal scaloppine
6 slices cooked ham
12 scallions
4 oz mature Gruyère cheese, cut into
12 sticks about ¼ inch wide
6 tablespoons butter
8 oz button mushrooms, sliced
½ cup dry white wine
salt and pepper
watercress sprigs, to garnish (optional)

place the scaloppine between sheets of wax paper and pound until thin. Cut each slice of ham in half. Place half a ham slice, a scallion, and a stick of Gruyère on each veal scaloppine and roll up. Tie with string or secure with wooden toothpicks.

melt the butter in a large frying pan. Add the veal olives and brown on all sides; remove from the pan as they brown.

add the mushrooms to the pan and fry for 5 minutes. Stir in the wine with salt and pepper to taste and bring to a boil. Return the veal olives to the pan and simmer, covered, for about 10 minutes, or until tender. Serve garnished with watercress sprigs, if using.

Serves 6
Preparation time: *30 minutes*
Cooking time: *25–30 minutes*

Scaloppine alla Bolognese

8 small veal scaloppine, about 3 oz each
flour, for coating
6 tablespoons butter
8 thin slices Parma ham
8 thin slices Gruyère or Emmenthal cheese
3 tablespoons Marsala
3 tablespoons Chicken Stock (see page 10)
salt and pepper

pound the scaloppine lightly with a rolling pin to flatten them. Sprinkle each one with a little salt and pepper, then coat them with flour.

melt the butter in a large frying pan and, when foaming, sauté the scaloppine for about 3–4 minutes on each side until they are browned and cooked. Arrange them side by side in a buttered ovenproof dish.

cover each scaloppine with a slice of ham and then top with a slice of cheese. Leave them in a warm place while you deglaze the pan.

add the Marsala and stock to the buttery juices in the pan and season with salt and pepper. Bring to a boil, scraping the bottom of the pan with a wooden spoon and stirring well. Spoon the sauce around the scaloppine in the dish and season with pepper. Place in a preheated oven at 450°F, or under the broiler for 5–10 minutes, until the cheese has melted. Add a few grindings of pepper and serve hot.

Serves 4
Preparation time: *10 minutes*
Cooking time: *about 15–20 minutes*
Oven temperature: *450°F*

Veal Scaloppine
with lemon and caper sauce

½ cup plain flour
8 thin veal scaloppine, total weight 1 lb
1½ tablespoons butter
2 tablespoons olive oil
zest and juice of 1 lemon
¾ cup dry white wine
2 tablespoons capers
salt and pepper

To serve
lemon wedges
fresh capers (optional)

put the flour into a large bowl, and season well with salt and pepper. Coat the veal scaloppine in the flour, and shake off any excess, reserving the excess flour.

heat the butter and oil in a large heavy pan. Add 2–3 veal scallops and cook in a single layer over a moderately high heat for 1–2 minutes on each side. Remove the veal from the pan, set aside and keep warm. Repeat with the remaining veal. Lower the heat if the butter starts to burn. Alternatively, drain the pan half-way through cooking and wipe clean with paper towels before heating more butter and oil.

remove all but 1 tablespoon of the butter and oil mixture from the pan. Add 2 teaspoons of the seasoned flour, mix well and cook until the mixture is well browned. Add the lemon zest, juice, and wine and stir until the mixture boils. Reduce the heat and simmer, uncovered, for 2 minutes.

add the capers and return the veal to the pan, turning the scaloppine quickly to coat with sauce, and cook for a further 1 minute. Serve immediately. Serve with lemon wedges and fresh capers, if available.

Serves 4
Preparation time: *20 minutes*
Cooking time: *about 10 minutes*

Veal Scaloppine al Basilico

16 small veal scaloppine
3 tablespoons flour
1 basil sprig
2 garlic cloves
6 tablespoons butter
½ cup dry white wine
½ cup water
salt and pepper
basil sprigs, to garnish

flatten the scaloppine with a rolling pin and coat lightly in the flour. Strip the leaves from the basil and chop roughly with the garlic cloves.

melt two-thirds of the butter in a large shallow pan over a moderate heat until foaming. Add the veal and cook for 1–2 minutes on each side then remove from the pan, set aside and keep warm. Add the wine and water to the pan and season with salt and pepper. Bring to a boil then reduce the heat and cook about 10 minutes, until the sauce is thick and smooth.

transfer the scaloppine to a warmed serving dish. Add the remaining butter to the pan, then the basil and garlic mixture. Cook, stirring, for about 1 minute, and pour over the veal. Serve accompanied by zucchini or a green salad.

Serves 8
Preparation time: *15 minutes*
Cooking time: *15–20 minutes*

Poultry & Game

Stuffed Chicken Breasts

4 boneless skinless chicken breasts

4 thin small slices Parma ham

4 thin slices Bel Paese cheese

4 cooked or canned asparagus spears

flour, for dusting

4 tablespoons butter

1 tablespoon olive oil

6 tablespoons Marsala or dry white wine

2 tablespoons Chicken Stock (see page 10)

salt and pepper

Italian parsley sprigs, to garnish

place each chicken breast between 2 sheets of wax paper and pound until thin. Season lightly with salt and pepper.

put a slice of Parma ham on top of each chicken breast, then a slice of Bel Paese and, finally, an asparagus spear. Roll each breast up and wind a piece of string around to hold it. Tie securely and dust with flour.

heat 2 tablespoons of the butter with the oil in a frying pan. Sauté the chicken rolls over a very low heat, turning them frequently, for about 15 minutes, or until tender, cooked, and golden. Remove the string, and transfer the rolls to a serving dish and keep warm.

add the Marsala or wine, chicken stock, and the remaining butter to the juices in the pan. Bring to a boil and simmer for 3–4 minutes, scraping the base of the pan with a wooden spoon to pick up all the juices. Spoon the sauce over the chicken, garnish with parsley sprigs, and serve with asparagus spears, if liked.

Serves 4
Preparation time: *20 minutes*
Cooking time: *about 30 minutes*

Chicken Cacciatore

3–4 tablespoons olive oil
3 lb chicken, cut in pieces
2 oz fat bacon, diced
1 onion, finely chopped
1 garlic clove, crushed
1 teaspoon flour
½ cup dry white wine
1 cup Chicken Stock (see page 10)
4 ripe tomatoes, skinned, deseeded, and sliced
1 teaspoon tomato purée
4 oz mushrooms, quartered
salt and pepper
chopped Italian parsley and parsley sprigs, to serve

heat 2 tablespoons of the oil in a casserole and brown the chicken pieces on all sides. Remove from the pan and add the bacon. Cook until golden brown, then remove from the pan. Add more oil if necessary and cook the onion and garlic gently until golden brown. Add the flour and cook together for a few moments, then stir in the white wine, stock, tomatoes, and tomato purée. Bring to a boil and season lightly.

return the chicken and bacon to the casserole. Cover tightly and cook in a preheated oven at 375°F for 25–30 minutes. Add the mushrooms and continue cooking for a further 10–15 minutes, until the chicken and mushrooms are tender.

put the chicken pieces on a warmed serving dish, cover and keep warm. If necessary, boil the sauce to reduce it to a coating consistency. Pour the sauce over the chicken, sprinkle with the parsley, and garnish with the parsley sprigs just before serving.

Serves 4
Preparation time: *25–30 minutes*
Cooking time: *about 1 hour*
Oven temperature: *375°F*

clipboard: You can use 4 chicken breasts or 8 thighs for this recipe. Chicken breasts will only need a total of 25–30 minutes to cook but thighs will need longer.

Tuscan Chicken
with polenta

4 tablespoons olive oil
1 chicken, cut into pieces
1 onion, chopped
5 plum tomatoes, skinned and chopped
1 cup dry white wine
1 rosemary sprig
1 tablespoon chopped thyme
1 tablespoon flour
1 tablespoon butter
salt and pepper
2 tablespoons chopped Italian parsley, to serve

Polenta
6 cups water
10 oz instant polenta flour
1 tablespoon butter

heat the olive oil in a large heavy frying pan and sauté the chicken pieces until golden brown all over, turning occasionally. Remove from the pan and keep warm.

add the onion to the pan and cook gently until soft and golden. Add the chopped tomatoes, white wine, rosemary, thyme, and salt and pepper to taste. Bring to a boil, stirring, and then reduce the heat to a simmer. Return the chicken to the pan and then simmer, covered, for 20–30 minutes until the chicken is cooked.

meanwhile, make the polenta. Heat the water to a gentle simmer, pour in the polenta flour and beat well for 1–2 minutes, until it is a smooth paste. Turn the heat down and continue to cook the polenta until it thickens, stirring constantly, for 6–8 minutes, until it is thick and smooth and has absorbed all the liquid. Stir in the butter and season with salt and pepper.

remove the chicken and arrange on a warmed serving dish. Blend the flour and butter (*beurre manié*) and add to the sauce. Bring to a boil, stirring constantly, until the sauce thickens slightly. Pour the sauce over the chicken, sprinkle with parsley and serve with the polenta.

Serves 4
Preparation time: *15 minutes*
Cooking time: *40 minutes*

Pollo alla Valdostana

6 part-boned chicken breasts

½ teaspoon dried oregano

½ teaspoon dried basil

2 tablespoons olive oil

3 slices Parma ham

2 garlic cloves, crushed

2 tablespoons balsamic vinegar

6 tablespoons dry Italian vermouth or dry white wine

3 thin slices Fontina cheese, about 3 oz in total

salt and pepper

basil sprigs, to garnish

sprinkle the opening in each chicken breast with the dried oregano and basil, and add salt and pepper to taste.

heat the oil in a large heavy pan. Add the chicken breasts and sauté over a moderate heat for 1–2 minutes on each side, until they just change color. Remove with a slotted spoon and leave until cool enough to handle. Reserve the oil.

cut the slices of Parma ham in half. Stuff each chicken breast with a piece of ham, then place the chicken breasts in a single layer in a lightly oiled ovenproof dish.

return the pan to the heat, add the garlic and balsamic vinegar, and stir until sizzling. Stir in the vermouth or wine and pour over the chicken breasts. Halve each slice of Fontina, and place a slice on top of each chicken breast.

put the chicken in a preheated oven at 400°F and cook for 20 minutes, or until the Fontina melts and the chicken is tender. Season with pepper and serve garnished with basil.

Serves 6
Preparation time: *15 minutes*
Cooking time: *about 25 minutes*
Oven temperature: *400°F*

Pot-roast Turkey

6 lb oven-ready turkey, giblets removed
2 tablespoons olive oil
1 tablespoon butter
4 tablespoons anise-flavoured liqueur
½ cup dry white wine
salt and pepper

Risotto Stuffing
2 tablespoons olive oil
1 onion, finely chopped
4 oz arborio rice
5 cups hot Chicken Stock (see page 10)
4 oz rindless pancetta, chopped
1 fennel bulb, finely chopped, with fronds reserved
2 garlic cloves, finely chopped
4 tablespoons grated Parmesan cheese
1 egg, beaten

first make the stuffing. Heat the oil in a saucepan and gently sauté the onion, stirring, until soft. Stir in the rice, add half of the stock and bring to a boil. Stir until the stock is absorbed, then add the remaining stock and return to a boil. Cover and simmer, stirring frequently, for 15 minutes or until all the stock is absorbed. Set aside.

fry the pancetta until the fat starts to run. Add the fennel, garlic, and pepper to taste and cook, stirring, for 10 minutes until soft. Add to the rice with half of the Parmesan and the egg. Stir, then leave to cool.

fill the neck end of the turkey with the stuffing, and truss with string. Place any leftover stuffing in an oiled baking dish and sprinkle with the remaining Parmesan. Heat the oil with the butter in a large flameproof casserole. Add the turkey and cook for about 10 minutes until lightly colored on all sides. Pour the liqueur over the turkey, allow to sizzle, then pour over the wine and season to taste.

cover and cook in a preheated oven at 350°F for 2½–3 hours until the juices run clear when the thickest part of a thigh is pierced with a skewer or sharp knife. Baste occasionally. Place the dish of stuffing in the oven for the last 15–20 minutes, until heated through.

remove the bird from the oven, and discard the trussing string. Cover tightly with aluminum and set aside to rest for about 15 minutes. Keep the cooking juices hot. Serve the turkey garnished with the reserved fennel fronds, with the cooking juices and any extra stuffing served separately.

Serves 6–8
Preparation time: *30 minutes, plus standing*
Cooking time: *3–3½ hours*
Oven temperature: *350°F*

Guinea Fowl
with mushrooms and gnocchi

1 plump guinea fowl, cut into 8 pieces

2 tablespoons seasoned flour

2 tablespoons olive oil

2 shallots, finely chopped

1 garlic clove, crushed

2 tablespoons chopped sage

1 cup dry white wine

1 cup Chicken Stock (see page 10)

1 bay leaf

salt and pepper

Gnocchi

1½ lb large potatoes, unpeeled

1 egg, beaten

3 tablespoons chopped Italian parsley

½ cup flour, sifted

Mushrooms

4 tablespoons butter

1 shallot, finely chopped

1 lb mixed wild or cultivated mushrooms, cut into halves or quarters if large

finely grated zest of 1 lemon

2 tablespoons lemon juice

roll the guinea fowl in the seasoned flour, shaking off any excess. Heat the oil in a large flameproof casserole, add the guinea fowl, in batches, and brown well all over. Remove with a slotted spoon and set aside. Reduce the heat, add the shallots, garlic, and sage and cook gently for 5 minutes until soft. Add the wine and bring to a boil, scraping up any residue from the bottom of the casserole. Return the guinea fowl and add the stock and bay leaf. Bring back to the boil, reduce the heat, cover and simmer gently for 25–30 minutes.

meanwhile make the gnocchi. Boil the potatoes, drain well and peel. While still warm, press through a sieve into a bowl. Beat the egg and parsley into the potato mixture. Add the flour a little at a time (you may not need it all) until the mixture is smooth and slightly sticky. Season with salt. Roll out on a lightly floured surface to form a long sausage ½ inch in diameter. Cut into ¾-inch lengths. Take one piece at a time and press it on to a floured fork. Roll along the prongs and off the fork on to a floured tray. Set aside.

to cook the mushrooms, melt the butter in a pan over a low heat, add the shallot and cook until soft. Add the mushrooms, lemon zest, and juice and cook until soft. Stir into the casserole for the last 10 minutes of cooking.

drop 20–25 pieces of gnocchi at a time into a large pan of boiling water. They will quickly rise to the surface. Cook for 10–15 seconds. Remove with a slotted spoon, drain, and keep warm while cooking the remainder. Discard the bay leaf, and serve the casserole with the gnocchi.

Serves 4
Preparation time: *45 minutes*
Cooking time: *about 1 hour*

Braised Pheasant
with Marsala and chestnuts

1 lb fresh chestnuts or 8 oz vacuum-
packed cooked chestnuts
1 tablespoon butter
2–2½ lb pheasant
4 oz pancetta or bacon, cut into strips
1 large onion, chopped
1 celery stick, chopped
1 large carrot, chopped
1 tablespoon chopped sage
¼ cup Marsala
2 cups game stock or Chicken Stock (see page 10)
salt and pepper

Beet straws
8 oz raw beets
oil, for deep-frying

cut a slash in the pointed end of each fresh chestnut, if using. Place the chestnuts in a saucepan, cover with water, bring to a boil and simmer for 2 minutes. Remove the pan from the heat. Using a slotted spoon, take out one chestnut at a time and remove the outer and inner skins.

melt the butter in a large flameproof casserole over a moderate heat, brown the pheasant all over, then transfer the bird to a plate. Reduce the heat, add the pancetta or bacon and cook for 1 minute. Add the onion, celery, and carrot and cook until the onion has softened.

return the pheasant to the pan and add the sage, Marsala, and stock, and the fresh chestnuts, if using. Season, bring to a boil, cover and simmer gently for 35–45 minutes until the pheasant and chestnuts are cooked. If using cooked chestnuts, add them after 20–25 minutes cooking.

make the beet straws: peel the beets and slice thinly, then cut the slices into matchstick-size strips. Place on paper towels and leave to dry for 30 minutes. Pat dry well. Heat the oil to 350–375°F, or until a cube of bread browns in 30 seconds. Cook the beet strips in batches until crisp; drain on paper towels.

remove the pheasant from the casserole and keep warm. Skim off any excess fat from the juices. Place over a moderate to high heat and boil rapidly until the sauce reduces and thickens slightly. Check the seasoning, then serve with the pheasant, accompanied by the beet straws.

Serves 4
Preparation time: *30 minutes, plus draining*
Cooking time: *1¼–1½ hours*

Quail *with peas and ham*

4 tablespoons butter
1 tablespoon olive oil
4–8 quails, cleaned and trussed
4 oz ham steak, finely diced
½ cup dry white wine
13 oz can tomatoes, drained, deseeded, and chopped
12 oz shelled fresh or frozen peas
½ cup Chicken Stock (see page 10) if needed
salt and pepper
chopped Italian parsley, to garnish

heat half the butter and the oil in a flameproof casserole and brown the quails on all sides. Remove from the pan and add half the diced ham. Cook until lightly colored, then return the quail to the pan with the wine and tomatoes. Season to taste and bring to a boil. Cover tightly and cook in a preheated oven at 375°F for 20–25 minutes until the quails are just tender.

meanwhile heat the remaining butter in a pan and cook the remaining ham until it is golden brown. Add the peas and, if necessary, a little water. Season lightly with salt and pepper. Simmer gently until the peas are tender and all the liquid has evaporated. Keep hot.

remove the cooked quails from the pan and remove any trussing strings. Place on a warmed serving dish and keep hot. Add the pea mixture to the pan and stir well over a gentle heat until the peas are coated with the sauce and are heated through. If necessary, add some chicken stock to the pan to give a coating consistency. Pile on the dish, garnish with chopped parsley, and serve at once with creamed potatoes.

Serves 4
Preparation time: *20–30 minutes*
Cooking time: *40–50 minutes*
Oven temperature: *375°F*

clipboard: If you are using fresh peas, choose young tender ones and add sufficient water to soften them but allow it almost to boil away by the time they are cooked. Frozen peas should need almost no water and will take only a few minutes to cook. Quails are very meaty little birds and you may find one is enough per person.

Braised Pigeon *with peas*

4 tablespoons olive oil
4 oz lean bacon, diced
1 onion, chopped
1 carrot, chopped
1 celery stick, chopped
1 garlic clove, chopped
4 young pigeons, cleaned
½ cup dry white wine
12 oz shelled fresh peas
pinch of ground cinnamon
3½ cups Chicken Stock (see page 10)
salt and pepper
rosemary sprigs, to garnish

heat the oil in a flameproof casserole, add the bacon, onion, carrot, celery, and garlic, and sauté gently for 10 minutes. Add the pigeons and fry until browned on all sides, turning frequently. Add the wine and cook until it has evaporated.

add the peas, cinnamon, salt, and pepper to taste, and the stock. Cover and simmer for 30 minutes or until the pigeons are tender, basting the pigeons with the cooking liquid occasionally. Serve hot, garnished with rosemary sprigs.

Serves 4
Preparation time: *15–20 minutes*
Cooking time: *about 50 minutes*

clipboard: Pigeons are most likely to be found in the frozen food section of the supermarkets. Thaw completely before cooking and use a boning or cook's knife to cut them in half.

Rabbit with Rosemary

simmered in red wine with olives

7 tablespoons olive oil

2½ lb wild rabbit, cut into serving pieces

2 garlic cloves, chopped

1 rosemary sprig, chopped

1 cup red wine

6–8 tablespoons Chicken Stock (see page 10)

2 tomatoes, skinned and mashed

8 oz black olives, halved and pitted

salt and pepper

heat the oil in a flameproof casserole, add the rabbit pieces and sprinkle with the garlic and rosemary.

sauté gently until the rabbit is browned on all sides, turning frequently.

add the wine and salt and pepper to taste. Cover and simmer for 30 minutes, adding a little stock to moisten as necessary.

add the tomatoes and olives and cook for a further 40 minutes until the rabbit is tender. Serve hot on a bed of tagliatelle.

Serves 4
Preparation time: *10minutes*
Cooking time: *1¼ hours*

clipboard: If you can obtain it, wild rabbit is best for this dish, as the flavor is stronger than farmed rabbit. Many of the larger supermarkets stock wild rabbit, otherwise look out for a butcher who specializes in game. If you can't get a wild rabbit, use a farmed one – it will taste milder, but is still very good.

Venison

with red currant sauce

1¼–1½ lb venison, diced
1 quantity Game Marinade (see clipboard, below)
2 tablespoons olive oil
4 oz piece rindless bacon, diced
2–3 tablespoons flour
6–8 tablespoons red currant jelly
2 tablespoons brandy
salt and pepper

To garnish
thyme sprigs
fresh red currants (optional)

place the venison and marinade in a bowl, cover and refrigerate for at least 24 hours, turning the venison from time to time. Remove the meat from the marinade and drain until dry. Reserve the marinade.

heat the oil in a casserole and sauté the bacon until golden brown. Remove from the pan. Season the flour well with salt and pepper and toss the venison in it. Add the venison to the pan and brown it on all sides in the hot oil. Add the bacon and the marinade. Season lightly, cover and simmer gently on top of the stove, or cook in a preheated oven at 350°F for 1½–2 hours.

remove the venison from the casserole, cover and keep warm. Strain the cooking liquid into a clean pan and whisk in 2 tablespoons of the red currant jelly. Boil until the sauce reduces to a thin coating consistency. Pour the sauce over the venison and keep warm.

melt the remaining red currant jelly in a small pan. Whisk until smooth. Add the brandy and boil for about 1 minute. Pour into a gravy boat and serve separately. Garnish with thyme and fresh red currants, if available.

Serves 4–6
Preparation time: *30–35 minutes, plus marinating*
Cooking time: *1¾–2¼ hours*
Oven temperature: *350°F*

clipboard: To make a game marinade, slice 1 carrot, 1 celery stick, and 1 large onion and crush 1–2 garlic cloves. Put them into a bowl with 2 cups red wine and add 6–8 parsley stalks, 1 sprig of thyme or rosemary, 2 bay leaves, 4 juniper berries, and 8 peppercorns.

Pizza, Rice, & Polenta

Basic Pizza Dough

The dried yeast used for this dough does not need pre-mixing with water, milk, or sugar and can be added directly to the flour. It is sometimes called easy-blend dried yeast, so read the package instructions carefully to ensure that you have the right one.

1 cup flour
1 envelope fast-action dried yeast
1 teaspoon salt
1 tablespoon olive oil
approx. ½ cup warm water

sift the flour, yeast, and salt into a bowl. Make a well in the center and add the oil. Gradually pour in the water, stir vigorously, bringing in the flour a little at a time, to form a soft dough. Knead for at least 10 minutes until the dough feels silky smooth and springy.

place the dough in an oiled bowl, turning once so the surface is coated. Cover the bowl with a cloth and leave to rise in a warm place for 1–2 hours until doubled in size.

when the dough has risen sufficiently, punch it down and turn it out onto a floured surface. Knead again for 2–3 minutes.

Makes enough for 1 x 12 inch pizza,
  2 x 8 inch pizzas,
  4 x 6 inch pizzas or
  6 x 5 inch pizzas
Preparation time: *15 minutes, plus rising*
Cooking time: *see recipes*

Pizza Napoletana

Fresh yeast is used for this pizza dough, but you can use the Basic Pizza Dough made with fast-action dried yeast on page 158 if you prefer.

½ oz fresh yeast
2 tablespoons warm water
1 cup flour
1 teaspoon salt
2 tablespoons olive oil
3 tablespoons milk
1 tablespoon torn basil leaves, to garnish

Topping
4 tablespoons olive oil
13 oz can chopped tomatoes, drained
1 tablespoon chopped basil
1 teaspoon dried oregano
6 oz mozzarella cheese, sliced
4 tablespoons grated Parmesan cheese
salt and pepper

blend the yeast with the warm water in a small bowl. Leave in a warm place for 10 minutes until frothy. Sift the flour and salt into a large bowl, make a well in the center and pour in the yeast mixture, oil, and milk. Gradually draw the flour into the liquid and mix to form a stiff but pliable dough, adding more milk if necessary.

knead the dough on a lightly floured surface for about 5 minutes, until it is light and elastic. Place in an oiled bowl, turning once so the surface is coated. Cover the bowl with a cloth and leave to rise in a warm place for 1 hour, or until doubled in size. Turn out onto a floured surface and divide into 2 or 4 pieces. Knead each piece lightly.

roll out the dough to cover two 9-inch or four 6-inch lightly oiled ovenproof plates. Alternatively, place a piece of dough on each plate and press it out, with floured knuckles, to cover the base.

brush with some of the oil, cover with the tomatoes, and season with salt and pepper. Sprinkle with the herbs, top with mozzarella, a sprinkling of Parmesan and a little more oil. Leave to rise in a warm place for 30 minutes. Bake in a preheated oven at 425°F for 15 minutes, then reduce the heat to 350°F for 5 minutes. Serve sprinkled with torn basil.

Serves 4
Preparation time: *15 minutes, plus rising*
Cooking time: *20 minutes*
Oven temperature: *425°F*

Many Tomato Pizza

This pizza is topped with a variety of different tomatoes which make an interesting contrast in colors and flavors.

1 quantity Basic Pizza Dough (see page 158), risen
extra virgin olive oil, for oiling and drizzling

Topping
2 large ripe plum tomatoes, skinned and sliced
10 red cherry tomatoes, skinned and halved
5 yellow pear tomatoes, skinned and halved
4 sun-dried tomatoes in oil, drained and chopped
handful of basil leaves, torn into pieces
2 teaspoons grated lemon zest
12 black olives, pitted
sea salt and pepper

knead the risen dough on a lightly floured surface, divide in half, and roll out each piece to a 9-inch round. Transfer to 2 oiled pizza plates or a large oiled baking sheet.

dry the tomato slices on paper towels. Arrange all the tomatoes over the pizzas, scattering the basil, lemon zest, and black olives on top. Season well and drizzle with a little extra olive oil.

place at the top of a preheated oven at 450°F for 20 minutes, until the bases are crisp and the tops golden. Serve at once.

Serves 2
Preparation time: *10 minutes,
 plus making the dough and rising*
Cooking time: *20 minutes*
Oven temperature: *450°F*

Spicy Hot Pizza

1 quantity Basic Pizza Dough (see page 158)
marjoram sprigs, to garnish (optional)

Topping
1–2 tablespoons olive oil
1 garlic clove, crushed
2–3 shallots, chopped
3 tomatoes, skinned, deseeded, and chopped
½ cup dry white wine
1 teaspoon dried mixed herbs
2 tablespoons butter
2 red onions, sliced
2–3 green chilies, cored, deseeded, and sliced lengthways
1 tablespoon chopped thyme
1 tablespoon chopped marjoram
2 oz mozzarella cheese, diced
salt and pepper

first make the topping. Heat the oil in a pan, add the garlic and shallots, and cook for about 5 minutes, until golden. Add the tomatoes, wine, and dried mixed herbs. Bring to the boil and cook rapidly for 20 minutes, until thickened. Season with salt and pepper to taste and leave to cool.

melt the butter in a pan, add the onions, and cook for 5 minutes until golden. Leave to cool.

knead the risen dough on a lightly floured surface, and roll out to two 9-inch rounds. Transfer to a large heated, oiled baking sheet. Spread the onions on the pizza bases and cover with the tomato mixture. Sprinkle with the chilies, thyme, marjoram, and mozzarella.

bake at once in a preheated hot oven at 425°F for 15–20 minutes, until the dough and topping are golden. Garnish with marjoram sprigs, if using, and serve immediately.

Serves 4
Preparation time: *20 minutes, plus making the dough, rising and cooling*
Cooking time: *40 minutes*
Oven temperature: *425°F*

Artichoke and Mushroom Pizza

1 quantity Basic Pizza Dough (see page 158), risen
basil leaves, to garnish

Topping
2 tablespoons tomato purée
4–6 tomatoes, sliced
2 tablespoons chopped basil
2 tablespoons chopped oregano
14 oz can artichoke hearts, drained and sliced
2 oz button mushrooms, sliced
3 tablespoons olive oil
2 tablespoons grated Parmesan cheese
2 tablespoons grated Cheddar cheese

knead the risen dough on a lightly floured surface, and roll out to a round. Transfer to a large oiled baking sheet. Spread the tomato purée thinly over the base. Arrange the tomatoes over the tomato purée and sprinkle with the basil and oregano. Place the artichokes and mushrooms on top and drizzle with the oil. Sprinkle with the Parmesan and Cheddar.

bake at the top of a preheated oven at 425°F for 15–20 minutes, until golden. Serve at once, garnished with basil leaves.

Serves 4
Preparation time: *10 minutes,
 plus making dough and rising*
Cooking time: *15–20 minutes*
Oven temperature: *425°F*

Herbs & Spices

Thyme

Garlic

Bay leaves

Lemon thyme

Cloves

Juniper berries   Oregano

Saffron

Italian parsley

Bay leaves
Woven into their victors'
crowns by the ancient
Romans, this powerful herb,
used fresh or dried, is part of
the classic herb bouquet.
Remove bay leaves from
dishes before serving.

Cloves
The dried unopened buds of
a tropical evergreen tree,
cloves, used whole or

ground, impart a strong,
sweet flavor.

Lemon thyme
A delightful herb with the
usual aromatic thyme flavor
overlaid with lemon.

Juniper berries
These purplish black
berries, used in making gin,
frequently feature in pork
and game recipes.

Garlic
A perennial herb belonging
to the onion family, garlic
appears extensively in
Italian cooking. Its flavor is
mild when harvested in
early summer, growing
sharper with age.

Oregano
Closely related to marjoram,
but stronger and more
pungent, oregano dries well.

Saffron
The most expensive spice in
the world, saffron is made
from the dried stigmas of
the *crocus sativus* and must be
hand picked. It gives an
incomparable flavor,
especially to fish dishes.

Thyme
An extremely useful herb,
and used both as part of the
traditional herb bouquet

and on its own. It is a robust
herb which can withstand
long cooking and grows
very well in pots.

Italian parsley
Sometimes called
continental parsley, this is
one of the most useful
culinary herbs and has a
better flavor than the
crinkly leaved version. It is
also rich in vitamins.

Rosemary

Fennel

Basil

Chilies

Nutmeg

Dill

Marjoram

Sage

Chilies

The hottest spice of all. On the whole, the smallest chilies are the hottest ones. The seeds are always the most fiery part of all.

Nutmeg

Available whole, to be used grated, or ground, the nutmeg with its beautiful sweet flavor is the seed of a tropical evergreen tree. It is frequently found in Italian cooking particularly in bechamel and other sauces.

Rosemary

One of the herbs that shouts Italy very loudly (the others are basil and sage). Often used with lamb and chicken, rosemary is a very aromatic and strongly flavored herb, so use with care. It dries very well.

Fennel

There are three types of fennel, two are grown primarily as a herb for their seeds and leaves and the third as a vegetable. Fennel has an aniseed flavour and goes well with fish.

Dill

A bright green feathery herb and very similar in appearance to fennel.

Marjoram

An aromatic herb with a sweet spicy flavor and very similar to oregano. Use with chicken, veal, pasta dishes, and tomatoes. Marjoram is best added at the end of cooking.

Basil

Possibly the most important herb in Italian cooking, basil has soft bright green leaves and a superb flavor. Best known as the unique ingredient in pesto and for its affinity with tomatoes.

Sage

A herb with gray-green leaves and a slightly bitter flavor. The Italians often use it with veal and calves' liver dishes and to flavor cheeses. Sage can stand up to long, slow cooking.

Rich Polenta Salad

2 cups water
5 oz instant polenta flour
2 tablespoons butter
8 oz goat cheese, rind removed, thinly sliced or crumbled
1 small radicchio head
4 oz arugula
3 tablespoons extra virgin olive oil
1 tablespoon balsamic vinegar
salt and pepper

heat the water to a gentle simmer, pour in the polenta flour, and beat well for 1–2 minutes until it is a smooth paste. Turn the heat down and continue to cook the polenta until it thickens, stirring constantly, for 6–8 minutes.

add the butter and season with salt and pepper; mix well. Place the polenta on a chopping board and spread to ¼ inch thick and allow to set for 5 minutes.

arrange the goat cheese on the polenta, then cut the polenta into bars or wedges. Place the polenta under a preheated broiler and cook until the cheese has melted and starts to bubble.

place the radicchio leaves and the arugula in a bowl. Add the oil and vinegar, and season with salt and pepper, then toss the leaves until coated. Arrange the salad leaves on individual plates and place the polenta bars or wedges on top.

Serves 4
Preparation time: *10 minutes*
Cooking time: *15–20 minutes*

Baked Polenta
with Fontina

Fontina is a semifirm and creamy cheese from the Val d'Aosta in northern Italy.

2 cups water
5 oz instant polenta flour
½ cup butter, plus extra for greasing
handful of marjoram, chopped
7 oz Fontina cheese, grated
salt and pepper

Sauce
3 tablespoons olive oil
2 garlic cloves, crushed and chopped
I onion, chopped
13 oz can chopped tomatoes
I thyme sprig
I teaspoon vinegar
I teaspoon sugar
salt and pepper

heat the water to a gentle simmer, pour in the polenta flour and beat well for 1–2 minutes until it is a smooth paste. Turn the heat down and continue to cook the polenta until it thickens, stirring constantly, for 6–8 minutes.

add the butter and chopped marjoram and season with salt and pepper. Mix well. Place the polenta on a chopping board, roll out to ¾ inch thick and allow to set for 5 minutes.

meanwhile make the sauce. Heat the olive oil in a saucepan, add the garlic and onion and sauté for 3 minutes. Add the tomatoes, thyme, vinegar, and sugar. Season with salt and pepper and simmer for 10 minutes over a moderate to high heat, until the tomatoes reduce to a thick sauce.

butter a shallow ovenproof dish, cut the polenta into squares, and line the bottom of the dish with half of the squares. Sprinkle over half of the grated Fontina. Spoon over half of the sauce and top with the remaining polenta. Add the remaining sauce and the remaining grated Fontina and bake in a preheated oven at 400°F for 10–15 minutes, until the cheese is golden and the sauce bubbling.

Serves 4
Preparation time: *10 minutes*
Cooking time: *30–40 minutes*
Oven temperature: *400°F*

Risi e Bisi

A risotto is usually very moist with a thick syrupy consistency, unlike a pilaff which is a dry mixture. This Venetian dish is even more liquid, rather like a very thick soup. It is served as a first course and not eaten as an accompaniment to a main meal.

6 tablespoons butter
4 oz piece bacon, diced
1 large onion, chopped
1 tablespoon chopped parsley
14 oz shelled or frozen peas
pinch of sugar
4½ cups Chicken Stock (see page 10)
12 oz arborio rice
4–6 tablespoons grated Parmesan cheese
salt and pepper

heat 2 tablespoons of the butter in a pan and cook the bacon until lightly colored. Add the onion and cook until soft but not colored. Stir in the parsley and the peas. Add a pinch of sugar and season lightly with salt and pepper, then cook for 2–3 minutes. If fresh peas are used, pour on half of the stock and cook gently for 10–15 minutes. If frozen peas are used, add all the stock to the pan and bring to the boil.

add the rice and mix well. Season to taste and simmer for 10–15 minutes until the rice is tender but firm to the bite. If necessary, add a little more stock or some water to keep the risotto moist. When the rice is cooked, check the seasoning and stir in the remaining butter and the Parmesan. Transfer to a warmed serving dish and serve hot.

Serves 4–5
Preparation time: *20–25 minutes*
Cooking time: *35–40 minutes*

Sage Risotto

Sage originated on the northern shores of the Mediterranean and has been used in Italian cooking since time immemorial.

3½ cups Vegetable Stock (see page 11)
2 tablespoons olive oil
2 tablespoons butter
1 shallot, finely chopped
12 oz arborio rice
¼ cup dry white wine
20 fresh sage leaves, finely chopped
2 tablespoons light cream
2 tablespoons grated Gruyère cheese
salt and pepper
sage leaves, to garnish

warm the stock in a pan over a very low heat and gradually bring to a boil. Heat the oil and butter in a large pan and add the shallot. Sauté over a moderate heat for about 4 minutes, until golden but not brown. Gradually add the rice, stir well and continue to cook for a few minutes.

add the wine and simmer until it has completely evaporated, then add the boiling stock a little at a time and cook, stirring frequently, for about 25 minutes, until the stock has all been absorbed and the rice is creamy. Taste and season if necessary.

add the sage leaves, cream, and Gruyère. Turn off the heat, cover the pan and leave the risotto to rest for a few minutes before serving, garnished with sage leaves.

Serves 4
Preparation time: *5 minutes*
Cooking time: *35–40 minutes*

Spinach and Lemon Risotto

3½ cups Chicken Stock or
Vegetable Stock (see pages 10 and 11)
½ cup butter
1 tablespoon olive oil
2 shallots, finely chopped
10 oz arborio rice
1 lb spinach, chopped
grated zest and juice of 1 lemon
½ cup grated Parmesan cheese
salt and pepper

heat the chicken or vegetable stock in a saucepan to a gentle simmer.

melt half the butter and the olive oil in another saucepan, add the shallots, and sauté for 3 minutes.

add the rice and stir well to coat the grains thoroughly. Add a ladleful of stock, enough to cover the rice, and stir well. Simmer gently and continue to stir as frequently as possible, adding more stock as it is absorbed, reserving a ladleful.

stir in the chopped spinach, lemon zest, and juice, reserving a little lemon zest for garnishing, and season with salt and pepper. Increase the heat, stir well, then add the remaining stock and butter. Allow to cook for a few minutes, then add half of the Parmesan and mix in well. Serve sprinkled with the remaining Parmesan and lemon zest.

Serves 4
Preparation time: *5 minutes*
Cooking time: *about 30 minutes*

Milanese Risotto

½ cup unsalted butter

½ onion, finely chopped

13 oz arborio rice

½ cup dry white wine

3½ cups Chicken Stock (see page 10) or Vegetable Stock (see page 11), kept simmering

¼ teaspoon saffron threads

4 oz fresh Parmesan shavings

salt and pepper

basil leaves, to garnish

melt half of the butter in a large, heavy pan, add the onion, season with a little pepper, and fry gently for about 5 minutes until softened.

add the rice and stir to coat thoroughly in the buttery mixture.

add the wine, a ladleful of the stock, and the saffron threads, and cook over a low heat, stirring until all the liquid is absorbed.

continue adding the stock in this way, a ladleful at a time, and stirring until absorbed. The risotto is ready when all the stock has been absorbed and the grains of rice are tender and the risotto creamy and moist without being "gluey." (This will take about 20–25 minutes.)

remove the pan from the heat, stir in the remaining butter and the Parmesan shavings, garnish with basil, and serve immediately.

Serves 4–6
Preparation time: *5–10 minutes*
Cooking time: *25–30 minutes*

Fish Risotto

4–6 tablespoons unsalted butter
1 large onion, finely chopped
4–5 cups Fish Stock (see page 11)
1 celery stick, sliced
1 thyme sprig
2 Italian parsley sprigs
½ teaspoon mace
1 small onion, peeled but left whole and studded with 2 cloves
12 oz–1 lb arborio rice
½ cup dry white wine
1 lb monkfish, haddock, halibut or other firm white fish fillets, skinned and cubed
2 small red mullet, heads and tails removed, cut into 1-inch slices (optional)
3–4 saffron threads (optional)
1 garlic clove, finely chopped
10 oz cooked unshelled shrimp
2 tablespoons grated Parmesan cheese, plus extra to serve
sea salt and white pepper
finely chopped Italian parsley, to garnish

heat 2 tablespoons of the butter in a large pan, add the onion and cook for 5–10 minutes, until soft but not colored.

meanwhile, pour the fish stock into another pan, then tie the celery, thyme, parsley, mace, and studded onion in a piece of cheesecloth and add to the pan. Bring just to boiling point, then keep at a gentle simmer.

add the rice (use the larger amount if omitting the mullet) to the onions, and stir until well coated. Pour in the wine, raise the heat a little, and cook for 3–4 minutes until the wine has almost evaporated.

add a ladleful of the hot stock to the pan and cook on a low heat for 2–4 minutes, until the stock is almost absorbed, then add another ladleful. Stir into the rice. Continue adding stock, a little at a time, and stirring often, until you have added about 1¾ pints. Add the monkfish and red mullet, if using, then a little stock, and cook for 4–5 minutes.

place the saffron, if using, in a small bowl, pour over 3–4 tablespoons of the stock. Stir quickly to start the colour running, then set aside.

melt 1 tablespoon of the butter in another small pan, add the garlic and shrimp, and cook for 3–4 minutes, then stir into the risotto. Add the saffron liquid, and another ladleful of stock if you have used the whole quantity of the rice. The rice should be tender and the risotto creamy and moist without being "gluey." Season with salt and pepper.

add the remaining butter and the Parmesan, stirring until melted, then heap into a warmed serving dish, sprinkle with parsley, and serve at once with more Parmesan.

Serves 6–8
Preparation time: *20 minutes*
Cooking time: *45–55 minutes*

Stuffed Rice Croquettes

4 cups water

½ cup meat gravy

3 tomatoes, skinned, deseeded, and chopped

4 tablespoons butter

1 lb arborio rice

6 tablespoons grated Parmesan cheese

3 eggs, lightly beaten

4 oz mozzarella cheese, diced

fine dry breadcrumbs, for coating

oil, for deep-frying

salt and pepper

Meat filling

4 tablespoons butter

2 slices Parma ham, shredded

1 small onion, finely chopped

4 oz chopped veal

2 tomatoes, skinned, deseeded, and chopped

4 oz chicken livers, chopped

salt and pepper

bring the water to the boil in a large pan. Stir in the gravy, tomatoes, and butter, and pour in the rice. Mix well and simmer over a low heat for 15 minutes, or until the rice is tender. Stir occasionally to prevent it sticking and add more water if necessary.

meanwhile, make the filling. Heat the butter in a saucepan over a moderate heat and sauté the ham and onion. Add the veal and cook until lightly browned. Add the tomatoes and simmer until reduced. Add the chicken livers and cook quickly. Season and remove the pan from the heat.

remove the rice mixture from the heat, and stir in the grated Parmesan and beaten eggs. Season with salt and pepper. Turn the rice mixture into a bowl and set aside to cool.

place a rounded tablespoon of rice in the palm of one hand. Make a depression in the center and fill with some of the meat mixture and 2 cubes of mozzarella. Cover the filling with the rice and shape into a ball. Repeat with the rest of the mixture and coat the rice balls with breadcrumbs. Heat the oil to 350–375°F, or until a cube of bread browns in 30 seconds, and deep-fry the rice balls, a few at a time, until golden brown. Drain on paper towels and serve hot.

Serves 4–6
Preparation time: *20 minutes*
Cooking time: *45 minutes*

Vegetable & Salad Dishes

Stuffed Zucchini

6 small zucchini, cut in half lengthways

2 tablespoons olive oil

I large onion, finely chopped

7 oz arborio rice

2 tablespoons butter

4–6 tablespoons grated Parmesan cheese

2 eggs

2 tablespoons milk

I tablespoon chopped Italian parsley

salt and pepper

cook the zucchini in a large pan of boiling salted water for 3–4 minutes. Drain well. Place under the cold tap until cool. Scoop out the seeds from each zucchini half with a teaspoon and discard.

heat the oil in a pan and cook the onion until it is soft and golden brown. Meanwhile, cook the rice in a large pan of salted boiling water for 12–15 minutes until tender but firm to the bite; drain well and place in a bowl. Stir in the butter, half of the Parmesan, and the onion. In another bowl, whisk together the eggs and milk and stir in the parsley and the remaining Parmesan. Season well with salt and pepper and stir into the rice mixture.

 place the zucchini halves in a well buttered ovenproof dish. Pile some of the rice mixture into each one and bake in a preheated oven at 400°F for 20–25 minutes until they are golden brown. Serve hot.

Serves 4
Preparation time: *25–30 minutes*
Cooking time: *35–40 minutes*
Oven temperature: *400°F*

clipboard: This dish can be served as an accompaniment to a main course or it makes a good appetizer.

Anchovy Stuffed Zucchini Flowers

Even if you do not have a garden, zucchini can be grown in window boxes very successfully. Some specialist stores and markets can supply the flowers in season.

8 zucchini flowers
8 anchovy fillets
vegetable oil, for deep-frying

Batter
1 egg yolk
1 tablespoon olive oil
½ cup light beer
¼ cup flour
1 tablespoon chopped basil
salt and pepper

first make the batter. In a large bowl, beat together the egg yolk, oil, beer, flour, and basil to make smooth batter. Season with salt and pepper. Cover and set aside for 30 minutes.

clean the courgette flowers carefully. Wash and dry the anchovies and slip an anchovy fillet into each flower.

heat 2 inches vegetable oil in a deep saucepan, until it reaches 350°–375°F, or until a cube of bread browns in 30 seconds.

dip the stuffed flowers into the batter two at a time. Deep-fry in the hot oil for 1–1½ minutes, until crisp and golden. Drain on paper towels and keep warm in a moderate oven while frying the rest. Serve hot.

Serves 4–8
Preparation time: *10 minutes, plus resting*
Cooking time: *6–8 minutes*

Vegetables & Leaves

Eggplant

Peppers

Globe artichoke

Vine tomatoes

Lollo rosso

Lollo bianco

Spinach

Globe artichoke
Usually eaten as an hors d'oeuvre, these are popular in Italy where they are also eaten in pies and frittatas.

Lollo rosso
A floppy lettuce with slightly bitter-tasting frilly leaves tinged with red.

Peppers
Also known as capsicums and bell peppers, these are part of the same family as chillies. Green peppers are red peppers in their unripe form.

Eggplant
These shiny vegetables are usually a glossy purple but a white variety is also available. Eggplant are usually diced, sprinkled with salt and left to drain for at least 30 minutes before cooking to get rid of their bitter juices. They are always cooked first but may be eaten hot or cold.

Lollo bianco
A small crinkly lettuce, similar to lollo rosso but with green leaves.

Vine tomatoes
Tomatoes, particularly the plum tomato, are one of Italy's great resources. The ones with the best flavor are those that have been slowly ripened on the vine, in the sun. Canned tomatoes are often the best alternative during the winter months.

Spinach
Young spinach, as shown above, can be eaten raw in salads. Spinach is an Italian

Fennel

Red onion

Garlic

Radicchio

Cherry tomatoes

Zucchini

Cavolo nero

Curly endive

Wild arugula

favorite, as a coloring for pasta as well as a vegetable.

Cherry tomatoes
The smallest and sweetest of tomatoes.

Curly endive
Also called frisée, this is a large, loose-headed lettuce-like member of the chicory family with a characteristic slightly bitter flavor.

Fennel
Its full name, Florence fennel, reveals its Italian origins. Italians eat it baked or braised with a sauce, or raw, sliced with a dressing.

Zucchini
A great favourite, cooked and eaten hot or cold. Zucchini flowers are also delicious stuffed.

Radicchio
Part of the chicory family, this salad leaf has red leaves patterned with white.

Wild arugula
A peppery and aromatic salad herb, sometimes called rocket, or found under its Italian name *rucola*.

Garlic
An essential flavoring in the Italian kitchen, where it is widely used.

Red onion
A mild member of the onion family.

Cavolo nero
A recent arrival, this very dark green, almost black, Italian cabbage is related to kale. It has a very strong flavor.

Eggplant Salad

This delectable salad can be served as an appetizer or as an accompaniment.

4 tablespoons olive oil
I onion, chopped
2 garlic cloves, crushed and chopped
2 eggplant, cubed
4 tomatoes, skinned and roughly chopped
4 anchovy fillets, chopped
2 tablespoons pitted black olives
½ cup pine nuts, toasted
2 tablespoons chopped capers
handful of Italian parsley, chopped
salt and pepper

Italian Salad Dressing

I tablespoon white wine vinegar
3 tablespoons olive oil
juice of ½ lemon
I teaspoon Dijon mustard
salt and pepper

heat the olive oil in a saucepan, add the onion, garlic, and eggplant, and sauté for 15 minutes.

meanwhile, make the Italian salad dressing. Place all the ingredients in a jar with a lid and shake well. Set aside.

add the tomatoes, anchovies, olives, pine nuts, capers, and parsley to the eggplant mixture and season with salt and pepper. Pour in the salad dressing, mix well then allow the salad to cool before serving.

Serves 4
Preparation time: *10 minutes, plus cooling*
Cooking time: *15 minutes*

Peperonata

Peppers, tomatoes, onions, and garlic braised in olive oil are the simple ingredients of this colorful Sicilian classic, although you could also add some chopped olives if you like. It is equally delicious served hot or cold.

½ cup olive oil
3 onions, finely sliced
2 garlic cloves, crushed
1 lb red and yellow bell peppers, cored, deseeded, and quartered
1 lb ripe tomatoes or 13 oz can chopped tomatoes
salt and pepper

heat the oil in a heavy saucepan and gently sauté the onions and garlic until they are lightly colored.

add the peppers, cover, and cook over a gentle heat for 10–12 minutes.

add the tomatoes and season generously with salt and pepper.

cook, uncovered, until the peppers are tender and the liquid has reduced to a thick sauce. Check the seasoning and pour into a serving dish.

Serves 4
Preparation time: *20 minutes*
Cooking time: *40–45 minutes*

clipboard: If you are using canned tomatoes, increase the heat toward the end of the cooking time so that the extra liquid evaporates. If you prefer, you can skin the peppers before you cook them.

Balsamic Braised Leeks and Peppers

Balsamic vinegar is regarded as the best and sweetest vinegar in the world. It comes from Modena where it is aged in wooden barrels for at least seven years and treated with all the reverence given to a leading château-bottled claret.

2 tablespoons olive oil
2 leeks, cut into ½-inch pieces
1 orange bell pepper, cored, deseeded, and cut into ½-inch chunks
1 red bell pepper, cored, deseeded, and cut into ½-inch chunks
3 tablespoons balsamic vinegar
handful of Italian parsley, chopped
salt and pepper

heat the olive oil in a saucepan, add the leeks and orange and red peppers and stir well. Cover the pan and cook very gently for 10 minutes.

add the balsamic vinegar and cook for a further 10 minutes without a lid. The vegetables should be brown from the vinegar and all the liquid should have evaporated.

season well, and stir in the parsley just before serving.

Serves 4
Preparation time: *5 minutes*
Cooking time: *20 minutes*

Cavolo Nero with Pancetta

1 tablespoon olive oil
1 onion, sliced
1 garlic clove, crushed and chopped
1 red chili, cored, deseeded, and diced
4 oz pancetta, diced
1 head cavolo nero
½ cup Chicken Stock (see page 10)
6 tablespoons coarsely grated Parmesan cheese
salt and pepper

heat the olive oil in a large saucepan, add the onion, garlic, chili, and pancetta and sauté for 5 minutes or until soft.

prepare the cavolo nero. Trim any wilting leaves then cut the head in half lengthways. Remove and discard the hard central stem and roughly chop the leaves.

add the cavolo nero to the onion mixture and stir well. Pour in the chicken stock and season with salt and pepper; cook for 4 minutes over a moderate heat, stirring all the time.

serve sprinkled with the grated Parmesan.

Serves 4
Preparation time: *5 minutes*
Cooking time: *10 minutes*

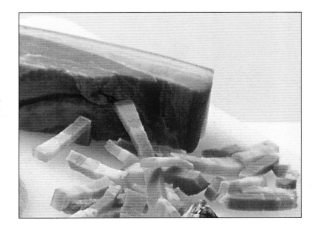

clipboard: Cavolo nero is a dark green Italian winter cabbage with long crinkly leaves. It becomes a brilliant green when cooked.

Mixed Grilled
Vegetables
with olive and walnut paste

Choose a selection of vegetables in season to serve with this rich green olive and walnut paste.

1 large eggplant, cut into ½-inch slices
2 red bell peppers, cored, deseeded, and halved, with stalks left on
2 yellow bell peppers, cored, deseeded, and halved, with stalks left on
2 zucchini, sliced lengthways
8 baby leeks, trimmed and cleaned
6 tablespoons olive oil
4 large slices crusty country bread
salt and pepper

Olive and Walnut Paste
3 oz pitted green olives
½ cup walnut pieces
2 tablespoons bottled pickled walnuts, drained
2 garlic cloves, chopped
small handful of parsley
½ cup extra virgin olive oil

first make the olive and walnut paste. Place the olives, fresh and pickled walnuts, garlic, and parsley in a food processor or blender and chop finely. Gradually add the olive oil through the feeder tube until the mixture forms a stiff paste. Scrape into a bowl and season with salt and pepper.

arrange the eggplant slices on a wire rack over a tray and sprinkle with 1–2 teaspoons salt. Leave for at least 30 minutes to drain; this removes some of the liquid and bitter flavor. Rinse thoroughly, drain well and dry on paper towels.

brush the eggplant, red and yellow peppers, zucchini, and leeks with the olive oil. Place on the greased grill of a preheated barbecue or under a broiler and cook the eggplant and peppers for 6–8 minutes, and the zucchini and leeks for 3 minutes, turning frequently, until tender. Brush the bread with any remaining olive oil and grill until golden. Spread the toast with the olive oil and walnut paste and top with the vegetables.

Serves 4
Preparation time: *30 minutes, plus draining*
Cooking time: *10 minutes*

Roasted Zucchini
with Gruyère and tomatoes

6 zucchini
4 tablespoons olive oil
¼ cup fresh breadcrumbs
4 tablespoons finely chopped basil
4 oz Gruyère cheese, cut into small cubes
8 oz cherry tomatoes, halved

cut the zucchini into 1-inch thick rounds. Using a melon baller, scoop out the center of each round but leave the bottom intact in each so the round is shaped like a cup.

heat the oil in a frying pan, add the breadcrumbs and cook, stirring, until golden and crunchy. Stir in the basil and set aside.

line a baking sheet with wax paper and arrange the zucchini rounds on it. Place a cube of Gruyère in each zucchini round and top with half a tomato. Bake in a preheated oven at 350°F for 5–7 minutes or until the courgettes are just tender.

serve sprinkled with the breadcrumb and basil mixture.

Serves 10 as an appetizer or
   accompaniment
Preparation time: *25 minutes*
Cooking time: *about* 10 *minutes*
Oven temperature: *350°F*

Potatoes Wrapped in Parma Ham

These delectable potatoes are equally good served as an accompaniment to a roast or nibbled as an appetizer with drinks. They are quite irresistible.

12 small new potatoes, cooked
12 very thin slices Parma ham
2 tablespoons olive oil
sea salt

roll each potato in a slice of Parma ham, patting with your hands to mould the ham to the shape of the potato.

oil a roasting pan, add the potatoes, and cook in a preheated oven at 400°F for 20 minutes. Check the potatoes once or twice while they are cooking and turn them, or move them around, to ensure they cook evenly.

serve the potatoes sprinkled with sea salt.

Serves 4
Preparation time: *10 minutes*
Cooking time: *20 minutes*
Oven temperature: *400°F*

Tortino alla Toscana

Tortino is the Tuscan version of a thick, flat omelet, traditionally made with globe artichokes. It is similar to a frittata, but is usually baked in the oven; it is not turned over during cooking or grilled at the finish.

4 baby globe artichokes
6 tablespoons olive oil
1 garlic clove, finely chopped
6 eggs
2 tablespoons finely chopped Italian parsley
salt and pepper

cut off and discard the tough ends of the artichoke stalks, if any. Pull off any coarse outer leaves, then cut across the tops of the leaves to neaten them. Cut the artichokes in half lengthways and remove any hairy chokes from the centers. Cut the artichokes lengthways again, into slices about ¼ inch thick.

heat the oil in a 9-inch frying pan with an ovenproof handle. Add the artichoke slices, garlic, and salt and pepper to taste. Cook over a low heat, stirring frequently, for 10 minutes, or until the artichokes are tender.

beat the eggs and parsley in a jug, then pour into the pan. Bake in a preheated oven at 350°F for 20 minutes or until set. Serve hot, sprinkled with plenty of black pepper.

Serves 4
Preparation time: *10 minutes*
Cooking time: *30 minutes*
Oven temperature: *350°F*

Finocchio alla Toscana

Anise-flavoured fennel is a great favorite in Italy. It makes a very good accompaniment to chicken and lamb.

4 fennel bulbs
1 thick lemon slice
1 tablespoon vegetable oil
2 tablespoons butter
4 tablespoons grated Parmesan cheese
salt and pepper
fennel fronds, to garnish (optional)

trim the fennel bulbs and remove any discolored skin with a potato peeler. Cut vertically into ¾-inch thick pieces. Place in a pan with a pinch of salt, the lemon, and oil and add sufficient boiling water to cover. Cook for 20 minutes or until just tender. Drain well.

melt the butter in a gratin dish or shallow flameproof casserole, add the fennel and turn to coat. Season to taste with pepper and sprinkle with the grated Parmesan.

place under a preheated broiler until lightly browned. Serve immediately, garnished with fennel fronds, if using.

Serves 4
Preparation time: *15 minutes*
Cooking time: *30 minutes*

Spinach with Egg

1 hard-boiled egg

1 lb spinach, shredded, or whole baby spinach leaves

2 tablespoons butter

grated nutmeg

1 tablespoon lemon juice

1 tablespoon olive oil

salt and pepper

cut the egg in half and remove and reserve the yolk. Chop the white.

wash the spinach well and place in a saucepan with just the water that clings to the leaves. Cover the pan and cook for 7–10 minutes, shaking the pan occasionally, until the spinach is tender. Drain the spinach well and return it to the pan with the butter and a sprinkling of nutmeg, and salt and pepper. Heat through, then remove from the heat and stir in the egg white, lemon juice, and olive oil.

transfer the spinach mixture to a warmed serving dish and sieve the egg yolk over the top. Serve hot.

Serves 4
Preparation time: *15 minutes*
Cooking time: *10–12 minutes*

Asparagus, Bean, and Pine Nut Salad

8 oz green beans
12 oz asparagus
3 slices brown bread
3 tablespoons olive oil
1 romaine lettuce
¼ cup toasted pine nuts
¼ cup freshly grated Parmesan cheese

Dressing

2 tablespoons olive oil
2 tablespoons cider vinegar
1 egg yolk
1 garlic clove, crushed

cut the beans and asparagus into 2-inch long pieces. Cook for 2 minutes in a large saucepan of boiling water. Drain and plunge into iced water. Drain again and wrap in a clean tea towel. Refrigerate until required.

remove the crusts from the bread and cut into ½-inch squares. Heat the oil in a frying pan, add the bread, and fry until the cubes are golden brown all over. Drain on paper towels.

wash and dry the lettuce. Arrange on a large platter. Combine the beans, asparagus, croutons, pine nuts, and Parmesan. Place on top of the lettuce.

to make the dressing, combine all the the ingredients in a screw-top jar. Shake well and pour over the salad. Serve immediately.

Serves 4–6
Preparation time: *20 minutes*
Cooking time: *5 minutes*

clipboard: Pine nuts are best toasted by placing them in a slow oven for 8–10 minutes. Cover the salad with dressing just prior to serving.

Desserts & Baking

Ice Cream Bombe

softened butter, for greasing
15–18 lady fingers
about ¾ cup brandy
1 container hazelnut ice cream
1 container chocolate ice cream
sifted cocoa powder and confectioners sugar, to decorate

grease the bottom of an 8-cup mold lightly with the softened butter, then place a circle of wax paper or nonstick parchment paper in the bottom.

check that the lady fingers are not too long to fit inside the mold and trim off the ends if necessary. Pour the brandy into a flat dish.

place one of the lady fingers in the brandy, turning it over several times until it is soaked. Work quickly, taking care that it does not break up. Stand the lady finger in the mold with the sugared side facing the mold. Repeat with the remaining lady fingers to make a solid lining, working as quickly as possible. Fill in the bottom of the mold with any broken lady fingers, also soaked in brandy. Chill in the refrigerator for at least 30 minutes.

spoon the hazelnut ice cream into the centre of the mold, then spread it up and around the side to cover the lady fingers completely. Freeze for about 2 hours until solid.

beat any remaining brandy into the chocolate ice cream, then use to fill the center of the pudding. Level the top, cover with aluminum foil and freeze until ready to serve.

remove the foil and carefully run a palette knife between the lady fingers and the mold. Invert a chilled serving plate over the pudding, then invert them both. Carefully lift off the mold and remove the wax paper circle. Decorate with cocoa powder and confectioners sugar and serve at once.

Serves 8
Preparation time: *45 minutes, plus chilling and freezing*

Torta della Nonna

Pastry

¾ cup flour

¼ teaspoon baking powder

pinch of salt

6 tablespoons sugar

finely grated zest of 1 lemon

½ cup chilled butter, diced

1 egg yolk

Filling

2 eggs

2 egg yolks

4 tablespoons sugar

4 teaspoons cornstarch

finely grated zest of 1 lemon

½ cup milk

½ cup heavy cream

confectioners sugar, to decorate

first make the pastry. Sift the flour, baking powder, and salt onto a cold surface and stir in the sugar and lemon zest. Make a well in the center and add the butter and egg yolk. Rub in with the fingertips until the mixture resembles fine breadcrumbs. Gather the dough together, then roll it out gently to a rough round on a lightly floured surface. Lift the round into a 9-inch fluted tart pan with a removable base and press the pastry into the corners and up the sides with your fingertips. Trim the top edge with a knife, then chill in the refrigerator for 30 minutes.

prick the bottom of the pastry all over with a fork, then line with aluminum foil and fill with baking beans. Place on a heated baking sheet in a preheated oven at 375°F, and bake blind for 15 minutes. Remove the foil and beans and set the pastry crust aside, still on the baking sheet. Reduce the oven heat to 325°F.

to make the filling, place the eggs, egg yolks, sugar, cornstarch, and lemon zest in a bowl and whisk well to mix. Heat the milk and cream in a heavy saucepan, until just below boiling point, then pour into the egg mixture, whisking all the time. Return to the pan and cook over a low heat until thickened, stirring constantly. Pour the custard into the pastry crust and bake for 30 minutes or until the filling is just set.

leave the tart in the tin until lukewarm, then place on a serving platter. Serve warm or cold, with confectioners sugar sifted over the top.

Serves 6
Preparation time: *40 minutes, plus chilling*
Cooking time: *45 minutes*
Oven temperature: *375°F*

Rags and Tatters

These carnival time fritters are popular in various regions of Italy where they are known by different names. The Tuscans call them cenci *because they are made from scraps, or bits and pieces, of dough.*

1 cup flour
1 teaspoon baking powder
¼ teaspoon salt
¼ cup butter
4 tablespoons superfine sugar
finely grated zest of 1 lemon
2 eggs, beaten
3 tablespoons sweet sherry
peanut oil, for deep-frying
confectioners sugar, to decorate

sift the flour, baking powder, and salt into a bowl, then rub in the butter with your fingertips. Stir in the sugar and lemon zest. Make a well in the center and add the beaten eggs and sherry. Mix with a wooden spoon until a dough starts to form, then gather the dough together with your hands, adding a little more sherry if the dough is too dry.

turn the dough out on a lightly floured surface and knead until smooth. Leave to rest in a cool place for 30 minutes.

divide the dough into manageable pieces. Roll out the pieces one at a time on a lightly floured surface until very thin, then cut into strips measuring about 3 x ¾ inches. Tie each strip into a knot.

heat the peanut oil in a deep-fat fryer until 350–375°F, or until a cube of bread browns in 30 seconds. Drop a few fritters into the hot oil and deep-fry for 1–2 minutes until golden and crisp. Lift out with a slotted spoon and drain on paper towels while deep-frying the remainder. Sift with confectioners sugar while still warm.

Makes about 50
Preparation time: *20 minutes plus resting*
Cooking time: *19–20 minutes*

Cassata alla Siciliana

3 eggs, separated
½ cup superfine sugar
finely grated zest of ½ lemon
3 tablespoons hot water
½ cup flour
I teaspoon baking powder

Filling

I cup superfine sugar
3 tablespoons water
1½ lb ricotta cheese
I lb mixed candied fruit
⅛ teaspoon ground cinnamon
3 oz unsweetened chocolate, chopped into small
pieces
8 tablespoons Maraschino liqueur

first make the sponge. Whisk the egg yolks with the sugar, lemon zest, and hot water, until light and foamy. Sift together the flour and baking powder and fold it gently into the egg yolk mixture.

whisk the egg whites until they are stiff, but not dry. Fold them into the sponge mixture. Pour the mixture into a buttered 10-inch springform cake pan and bake in a preheated oven at 375°F for 15–20 minutes, or until the cake is golden and springs back when pressed. Turn the cake out and cool on a wire rack.

to make the filling, dissolve the sugar in the water over a low heat. Beat the syrup with the ricotta until well blended. Chop half of the candied fruit coarsely. Beat the cinnamon into the ricotta mixture, and put aside a few tablespoons for decoration. Stir the chopped fruit and chocolate into the rest of the mixture.

line the base of the cake pan with wax paper. Cut the sponge in half horizontally and place one layer on the base, cut-side up. Sprinkle with half of the Maraschino, and spread with the ricotta mixture. Place the other sponge layer on top and sprinkle with the remaining Maraschino. Fit the ring of the pan in position and chill for several hours. To serve, remove from the pan, coat the top and sides with the reserved ricotta mixture, and decorate with the remaining candied fruit.

Serves 6–8
Preparation time: *40 minutes, plus cooling and chilling*
Cooking time: *15–20 minutes*
Oven temperature: *375°F*

Tiramisú

Mascarpone cheese is the Italian answer to clotted cream, and Tiramisú is one of the most popular dessert recipes using it. If you like, you can decorate the top with grated chocolate as well as the cocoa.

2 egg yolks
2 tablespoons superfine sugar
few drops vanilla extract
8 oz mascarpone cheese
¾ cup strong black coffee
2 tablespoons Marsala
1 tablespoon brandy
5 oz lady fingers
1 tablespoon cocoa powder

mix together the egg yolks and sugar in a bowl, beating with a wooden spoon until they are creamy. Add the vanilla extract and fold in the mascarpone. The mixture should be thick and creamy.

make the strong black coffee, then mix it with the Marsala and brandy in a bowl. Quickly dip the lady fingers in the coffee mixture. They should absorb just enough liquid to flavor them without going soggy and falling apart.

arrange some of the soaked lady fingers in the base of a large attractive glass serving bowl or 4 individual serving dishes. Cover with a layer of the mascarpone mixture.

continue making alternate layers of lady fingers and mascarpone, finishing with a layer of mascarpone. Sift the cocoa over the top, then chill in the refrigerator for 3–4 hours or until set. The flavor improves if the tiramisú is left overnight.

Serves 6
Preparation time: *20 minutes, plus chilling*

Tiramisú Gâteau

In Italian, tiramisú means "pick me up" – it's so indulgent!

6 tablespoons self-rising flour, sifted, plus extra for dusting
4 eggs, separated
2 tablespoons confectioners sugar, sifted
2 teaspoons plus 1 tablespoon instant coffee , sifted
¼ cup ground pecans
4 tablespoons chocolate-flavoured liqueur
2 tablespoons cocoa powder, sifted
8 oz unsweetened chocolate, melted

Mascarpone Custard

8 oz mascarpone cheese
3 teaspoons confectioners sugar
1 cup heavy cream, whipped

grease two shallow 8-inch round cake pans and line with greased wax paper. Dust with flour. Beat the egg whites to firm peaks. Gradually add the sugar; beat until it has dissolved and the mixture is glossy and thick. Add the egg yolks and beat for 20 seconds. Fold in the flour, 2 teaspoons coffee powder, and ground pecans. Spread into the pans. Bake in a preheated oven at 350°F for 15 minutes until lightly golden. Stand for 5 minutes. Turn on to a wire rack.

to make the mascarpone custard, beat the mascarpone and confectioners sugar until smooth. Fold in the cream.

line a deep 8-inch round springform pan with aluminum foil. Insert the first sponge. Brush with half the liqueur. Combine the cocoa and 1 tablespoon coffee powder, and dust half the mixture over the cake. Top with two-thirds of the mascarpone custard. Lay the second sponge on top. Brush with the remaining liqueur, and dust with the remaining cocoa mixture. Cover the cake and the remaining custard with plastic wrap, and refrigerate overnight.

line a 12- x 8-inch pan with foil. Spread the melted chocolate over. Refrigerate until semi-set. Cut circles of chocolate with a 2-inch round pastry cutter. Refrigerate until set. Remove the cake from the pan. Spread the remaining mascarpone custard around the side and press on the chocolate circles.

Serves 6–8
Preparation time: *1½ hours, plus chilling*
Cooking time: *15 minutes*
Oven temperature: *350°F*

Baked Stuffed Peaches

This recipe comes from Piedmont, in northern Italy, which is famed for its peaches.

4 large ripe peaches, halved and pitted
8 macaroons, crushed
4 blanched almonds, chopped
4 tablespoons superfine sugar
2 tablespoons cocoa powder
7 tablespoons dry white wine
3 tablespoons butter
flaked almonds
confectioners sugar, to decorate

scoop a little flesh from the centre of each peach half, chop and place in a bowl. Add the crumbled macaroons, almonds, half of the sugar, the cocoa, and 1 tablespoon of the wine. Fill the peach halves with the mixture and top each one with a small piece of butter.

arrange the peach halves in an ovenproof dish, pour the remaining wine over them, sprinkle with the remaining sugar, and top with a few flaked almonds. Bake in a preheated oven at 350°F for 25–30 minutes, or until the peaches are tender. Serve hot, sprinkled with confectioners sugar.

Serves 4
Preparation time: *15 minutes*
Cooking time: *25-30 minutes*
Oven temperature: *350°F*

Italian Cheeses

Fontina

Parmesan

Pecorino

Bel Paese

Taleggio

Provolone

Fontina

A table cheese from the Val d'Aosta in northern Italy, Fontina is reminiscent of Swiss Gruyère, but softer and sweeter and with smaller holes. Made from cow's milk, it melts well and so can be used for cooking as well as eating.

Bel Paese

This mild soft cream cheese was first produced in Lombardy in the 1920s and is now made all over Europe.

Parmesan

A hard, grainy textured cheese used for grating. Only cheeses from the town of Parma in Emilia-Romagna are true Parmesan and bear the official stamp *"parmigiano-reggiano"* on their rinds. Buy in a block and store in the refrigerator.

Taleggio

A cow's milk cheese from northern Italy, which is similar in taste and texture to a mild Camembert.

Pecorino

This sheep's milk cheese is usually hard and sharp, as shown above, but it can also be soft and mild, as seen above right. When hard, it is similar to Parmesan and also used for grating and in cooking.

Provolone

A cow's milk cheese, originally from the south, which may be mild or piquant. Mature provolone is used in cooking, young provolone as a dessert cheese.

Mozzarella

Pecorino

Bocconcino

Gorgonzola and
mascarpone tart

Ricotta

Dolcelatte

Mozzarella

A white curd cheese, originally made from buffalo's milk, with a soft chewy texture and a mild milky flavor. It is eaten fresh or used in cooking, particularly for pizza-making because of its excellent melting qualities.

Ricotta

A soft, very white fresh cheese made from the "re-cooked" whey of sheep's or cow's milk. Ricotta is used extensively in cooking, especially for desserts and baking. It is sold loose, cut from a round cake shape, or in plastic tubs.

Bocconcino

A fresh unripened cheese, shaped into small round balls, and sometimes referred to as baby or mini mozzarella. Bocconcino can be bought in plastic bags, packed in whey, with or without herbs. Store in the whey, in the refrigerator.

Dolcelatte

A soft, creamy blue-veined cheese (its name means sweet milk), dolcelatte is a mild mass-produced version of Gorgonzola. Although it doesn't claim the classic status of that great cheese, it is extremely pleasant in its own right.

Gorgonzola and mascarpone tart

A comparatively recent development, this is a very rich dessert cheese made of alternate layers of Gorgonzola and mascarpone. Because it is so rich, it is best eaten in small quantities.

Panettone Pudding

Panettone is a sweet yeast bread which Italians serve at Christmas. This recipe turns it into a version of bread and butter pudding.

¼ cup butter
5 slices panettone
apricot jam, for spreading
1 cup milk
1 cup heavy cream
2 eggs
1 egg yolk
¼ cup brown sugar, plus extra for the crust

butter a 4-cup ovenproof dish. Spread the panettone slices with the apricot jam and cut them into triangles or rectangles. Place in the buttered dish in overlapping layers.

pour the milk and cream into a saucepan and bring gently to the boil.

whisk together the eggs, egg yolk and sugar in a bowl until creamy and fluffy. Continue whisking and slowly add the hot milk and cream. When it is all combined, carefully pour it over the panettone, making sure that the custard mixture covers it. Sprinkle with a little extra sugar to make a nice crunchy crust.

fill a roasting pan with boiling water to make a water bath (*bain-marie*). Place the pudding in the *bain-marie* and bake in a preheated oven at 350°F for 25 minutes, or until the custard is set.

Serves 4
Preparation time: *15 minutes*
Cooking time: *30 minutes*
Oven temperature: *350°F*

Lemon Polenta Syrup Cake

¼ cup butter
¾ cup superfine sugar
½ cup ground almonds
¼ cup slivered almonds
½ teaspoon vanilla extract
2 large eggs
finely grated rind and juice of 1 lemon
3 oz instant polenta flour
½ teaspoon baking powder
cream, to serve

Syrup
grated rind and juice of 2 lemons
¼ cup superfine sugar
2 tablespoons water

line a 15 cm/6 inch cake tin with parchment paper.

beat together the butter and sugar until light and creamy. Add the ground and flaked almonds, vanilla extract and eggs and mix well.

add the lemon rind and juice, polenta flour and baking powder and mix well. Spoon into the prepared tin and bake in a preheated oven at 350°F for 25 minutes.

meanwhile make the syrup. Put the lemon rind and juice, sugar and water in a saucepan and heat through. Spoon over the cake as soon as it comes out of the oven. Allow the syrup to drizzle through. Serve the cake hot or cold with light cream.

Serves 4
Preparation time: *5 minutes*
Cooking time: *25 minutes*
Oven temperature: *350°F*

clipboard: Polenta is made from cornmeal. Formerly a staple food for the peasants of northern Italy, it became fashionable in the late eighties. In the past it required about 45 minutes constant stirring, but instant polenta has reduced its preparation time to almost nothing.

Strawberry Water Ice

1 lb strawberries
4 tablespoons orange juice
10 tablespoons sugar
4 tablespoons water
mint sprigs, to decorate

press the strawberries through a sieve, using a wooden spoon, reserving 4 whole ones for decoration. Stir in the orange juice.

gently heat the sugar and water, stirring, until the sugar has dissolved. Boil for 5 minutes, until syrupy. Cool, then stir into the strawberry pulp. Pour the strawberry mixture into a shallow container and freeze for 3–4 hours, until firm. Transfer the water ice to the refrigerator 30 minutes before serving.

slice the reserved strawberries in half lengthways. Serve the water ice in scoops decorated with the reserved strawberries and mint sprigs.

Serves 4
Preparation time: *10 minutes, plus freezing*
Cooking time: *5–10 minutes*

clipboard: When strawberries are out of season frozen ones can be substituted, although the flavour will not be as good. Choose a brand containing a minimum of sugar.

Macedonia di Frutta al Strega

Strega is one of the most popular of the Italian liqueurs; it is made from a delicate blending of different herbs, and has a distinctive vanilla flavour. Its deep golden colour lends a rich glow to fresh fruit salads.

1 cup dry white wine
½ cup sugar
grated rind of ½ lemon
4 tablespoons Strega liqueur
2 large ripe peaches
6 ripe apricots
4 large ripe plums
8 small fresh purple figs

Ricotta Cream
4 oz ricotta or cottage cheese
4 tablespoons whipping cream
2 tablespoons Strega liqueur

put the wine into a saucepan with the sugar and lemon rind. Stir over a gentle heat until the sugar has dissolved. Allow the syrup to cool, then stir in the Strega.

cut a small cross in the stalk ends of the peaches and apricots; scald in boiling water for 30 seconds and slip off the skins. Cut the peaches, apricots and plums around the middle and twist to separate the 2 halves, discarding the pits. Cut the peach halves into slices. Cut the figs into quarters lengthways. Add the prepared fruits to the Strega syrup, stirring them until evenly coated. Chill, covered, for 1 hour.

to make the ricotta cream, sieve the ricotta or cottage cheese and beat in the cream and the Strega. Cover and chill for 1 hour. Serve the fruit salad with the ricotta cream.

Serves 4–6
Preparation time: *30 minutes, plus cooling and chilling*
Cooking time: *about 5 minutes*

Chocolate Risotto

Serve this chocolate risotto in coffee cups in the authentic Italian style. Use a good quality dark chocolate with a high percentage of cocoa butter.

2 cups milk
2 tablespoons sugar
4 tablespoons butter
½ cup arborio rice
6 tablespoons hazelnuts, toasted and chopped
½ cup white sultanas
4 oz good quality unsweetened chocolate, grated
1 teaspoon brandy (optional)
grated chocolate, to decorate

put the milk and sugar into a saucepan and heat to simmering point.

melt the butter in a heavy saucepan, add the rice and mix well to coat the grains.

add a ladleful of the hot milk and stir well. When the rice has absorbed the milk, add another ladleful. Continue to stir and keep adding the milk until it is all absorbed. The rice should be slightly firm to the bite and with a creamy sauce.

add the hazelnuts, sultanas and grated chocolate and mix quickly. Serve decorated with a little grated chocolate. Try not to over-mix the grated chocolate as the marbled effect looks good. Add the brandy, if using, just before serving.

Serves 4
Preparation time: *5 minutes*
Cooking time: *20 minutes*

Mascarpone and Date Tart

This delightful dessert is a combination of soft cheese mixed with fruit.

1 cup flour
½ cup sugar, plus 2 tablespoons
6 tablespoons chilled butter
3 egg yolks
1½ cups fresh dates, halved and pitted
8 oz mascarpone cheese
½ cup heavy cream
2 eggs, lightly beaten
1 tablespoon cornstarch
2 teaspoons vanilla extract

grease a 9 inch fluted flan tin. Combine the flour, the ½ cup sugar, butter, and egg yolks in a food processor and blend until the mixture just comes together. Turn the mixture out on to a lightly floured surface, and press together until smooth. Roll the dough, between two sheets of plastic wrap, so that it is large enough to cover the tin base and sides. Ease into the tin and trim the edges. Chill for 20 minutes.

cut a sheet of wax paper to cover the pastry-lined tin. Spread a layer of baking beans over the paper and bake in a preheated oven at 350°F for 10 minutes. Remove from the oven, and lift off the paper and baking beans. Return to the oven for 10 minutes until the tart is golden. Cool.

place the dates over the pastry base. Combine the mascarpone, cream, eggs, the 2 tablespoons sugar, cornflour and vanilla essence in a bowl and whisk until smooth. Pour the mixture into the pastry shell and bake for 35 minutes or until the filling is golden and set.

Serves 8
Preparation time: *30 minutes, plus chilling*
Cooking time: *55 minutes*
Oven temperature: *350°F*

Stiacciata Unta

This Florentine sweetbread is a modern version of an ancient recipe. Stiacciata *means "squashed," referring to the fact that the bread is flat. It is eaten at carnival time in February.*

3½ cups flour
½ teaspoon salt
1 envelope fast-action dried yeast
½ cup superfine sugar
6 tablespoons unsalted butter, at room temperature
2 egg yolks
1 cup warm water
¼ cup orange juice
finely grated rind of 2 large oranges

To glaze
4 tablespoons unsalted butter, softened
confectioners sugar

brush a 12 x 10 inch roasting pan lightly with oil. Sift the flour and salt into a large warmed bowl, stir in the yeast and sugar, then rub in the butter with your fingertips. Stir in the egg yolks with a fork and make a well in the center.

mix the water and orange juice with the orange rind. Gradually work the liquid into the flour mixture, then turn out on a lightly floured surface and knead for about 10 minutes until smooth and elastic. The dough is quite sticky, so work a little more flour into it as you knead, but take care not to add too much or the finished bread will be dry and tough.

turn the dough into the pan and stretch and pull it to fit the tin evenly. Wrap closely and leave to rise in a warm place for 1–1½ hours or until the dough is doubled in size. Unwrap.

bake in a preheated oven at 350°F for 30–35 minutes until golden brown. Remove the bread from the oven, brush with the softened butter and sift icing sugar liberally all over the top. Leave to cool in the tin for 20–30 minutes, then cut into rectangles and sift over more icing sugar if you like. Serve warm.

Makes 16 rectangles
Preparation time: *30 minutes, plus rising and cooling*
Cooking time: *30–35 minutes*
Oven temperature: *350°F*

Garlic Focaccia

Panne all'pilo, *Italian olive oil bread has become universally popular. It is healthy and delicious, and not at all difficult to make — try this garlic-flavoured version.*

1 envelope dried yeast
1 teaspoon sugar
2½ cups plain flour
¾ cup warm water
1 teaspoon salt
3 garlic cloves, crushed
2 tablespoons olive oil
1 tablespoon corn meal or semolina
1 tablespoon olive oil, plus extra for glazing
2 teaspoons finely crushed sea salt

combine the yeast, sugar, 1 teaspoon flour, and the water in a small bowl. Stand, covered, in a warm place for 10 minutes or until foamy.

sift the remaining flour and salt into a large bowl. Add the garlic and stir with a knife to combine. Make a well in the center, stir in the yeast mixture and olive oil. Using a flat-bladed knife, mix to a firm dough.

turn out the dough on to a lightly floured surface, and knead for 10 minutes. Shape into a ball, and place in a large, lightly oiled mixing bowl. Stand, covered, in a warm place for 40 minutes or until well risen.

sprinkle the base of a 7 x 11 inch shallow baking pan with corn meal. Knead the dough for 2 minutes or until smooth. Press the dough into the tin, and prick deep holes in the dough with a skewer. Sprinkle lightly with water and place in a preheated oven at 400°F. Bake for 10 minutes and sprinkle again with water. Bake for a further 10 minutes, brush with extra olive oil, sprinkle with the sea salt, then bake for 5 minutes. Serve warm or at room temperature, cut into squares.

Serves 4–6
Preparation time: *20 minutes, plus rising*
Cooking time: *25 minutes*
Oven temperature: *400°F*

Olive Bread

1 envelope dried yeast
1¾ cups warm water
5 cups flour
2 teaspoons salt
4 tablespoons olive oil
4–6 oz black olives, pitted and roughly chopped

sprinkle the dried yeast over the water in a small mixing bowl. Set aside in a warm place until foamy.

sift the flour and salt into a large mixing bowl and make a well in the center. Pour in the yeast liquid with the olive oil. Mix well with your hand, drawing in the flour from the sides of the bowl, to form a dough.

place the dough on a lightly floured surface and knead well for 5–10 minutes, until the dough is elastic and smooth. Fold the dough inwards towards you with one hand while pushing it away with the other. Give it a quarter-turn and repeat. Put the dough in an oiled bowl, cover and leave in a warm place to rise until it has doubled in size.

punch down the dough to remove the air bubbles. Sprinkle with the olives and knead again. Divide the dough into 2 pieces and shape each one into a round loaf. Place on a greased baking sheet, cover with a cloth and leave in a warm place to rise again. Bake in a preheated oven at 450°F for 15 minutes and then lower the temperature to 400°F for a further 15 minutes. Cool on a wire rack and serve sliced.

Makes 2 loaves
Preparation time: *20 minutes, plus rising and cooling*
Cooking time: *30 minutes*
Oven temperature: *450°F*

Index

Acknowledgments

Photo Credits
Sean Myers: front jacket, front flap, back flap
Graham Kirk: back jacket

Special photography by Graham Kirk

All other photos:
Reed Consumer Books Ltd. / Bryce Attwell, Jean Cazals,
Gus Filgate, David Gill, Robert Golden, James Jackson,
Graham Kirk, Sandra Lane, William Lingwood, David Loftus,
James Merrell, Diana Miller, Hilary Moore, James Murphy,
Peter Myers, Sean Myers, Alan Newnham, Philip Webb,
Paul Williams

Front Jacket Home economist: Oona van den Berg
Home economist: Debbie Miller